INSECTS AND THEIR YOUNG

INSECTS AND THEIR YOUNG

Ross E. Hutchins

ILLUSTRATED WITH PHOTOGRAPHS BY THE AUTHOR

737

DODD, MEAD & COMPANY · NEW YORK

Frontispiece: Worker termites and a large-headed soldier
(center). Individuals of these castes never acquire wings
and may be of either sex. (Life size: ⅛ inch)

Library of Congress Cataloging in Publication Data

Hutchins, Ross E.
    Insects and their young.

    Includes index.
    SUMMARY: Divides insects into four categories,
according to their developmental stages, and discusses
their habits and characteristics.
    1. Insects—Development—Juvenile literature.
[1. Insects] I. Title.
QL495.5.H87   595.7'03   74-20862
ISBN 0-396-07062-0

INTRODUCTION

No writer of science fiction could dream up tales half as strange as the real-life stories of many insects. Take the seventeen-year cicada, for example. These remarkable insects insert their eggs in the twigs of trees. When these eggs hatch, the young cicadas drop to the ground and burrow in. As time passes they tunnel deeper and deeper into the earth until they may be several feet below the surface. Here in the darkness they live by sucking out the sap of roots and grow slowly. So slowly do they grow that seventeen years are required for the completion of their development.

As the summers pass, the young cicadas continue to siphon out the sap of roots and to increase in size. Each autumn the trees stop growing and the nutritious sap stops flowing through their roots. At this time the young cicadas stop feeding and become dormant. Winter's cold settles over the land and the ground becomes blanketed with snow. In time, spring arrives and the trees revive, unfolding new leaves. Deep in the earth, sap again flows through the roots and the young cicadas commence feeding once more. They resume their growth.

And so, for seventeen years the young cicadas gradually increase in size, feeding during the summers and resting during the long winters. When the seventeenth spring arrives, the cicada young, now fully developed, and more than an inch long, tunnel up toward the earth's surface and, shortly, emerge into the sunlit world they left so many years ago. Each young cicada slowly crawls up a tree and anchors its feet in the bark. After awhile a slit opens down its back and out crawls an entirely new and different kind of insect. It now has wings, soft and crumpled, but soon they expand and harden and the cicada has become an adult. It has been quickly transformed from an ugly creature fitted for tunneling in the earth into a creature fitted for flight. By means of complex drumming organs it will sing for a few weeks in the summer sun and the females will eventually lay their eggs in the twigs of trees. When these eggs hatch, the long life story will start over again. On another spring day, seventeen years in the future, another generation of cicadas will creep out of hidden tunnels to sing, mate, and lay eggs. Timed exactly by "clocks" within their bodies, they will "know" when the time has arrived to tunnel upward into the light of day. Here, certainly, is mystery beyond our understanding.

The life stories of many other insects are nearly as remarkable. In the pages that follow are recounted the ways various insects grow to maturity. Truly, they are stranger than fiction.

CONTENTS

In our discussions of the life stories of insects it will be helpful if we know a little about the way in which insects—as well as other animals—are classified. Insects belong to the large animal group known as the *phylum* Arthropoda, a Greek term meaning "joint-footed." To this same group also belong spiders, crabs, centipedes, millipedes, and some other creatures. Insects, however, are a special kind of arthropod, classified in the *class* Insecta or, sometimes, as Hexapoda or six-legged arthropods. The class Insecta is, in turn, divided into a number of *orders* which constitute the major divisions of the insect clan. Each order is made up of several *families* and these contain many *genera* (singular: *genus*). Each genus, in turn, contains many *species*.

The above scheme of classification was developed by Carolus Linnaeus, the great naturalist of Sweden (1707-1778) and published in his *Systema Naturae* in 1735. It is now followed by all biologists in dealing with both plants and animals.

To summarize the Linnean system of classification the following is given for the classification of the common tiger swallowtail butterfly:

Kingdom—Animal
Phylum—Arthropoda
Class—Insecta

Order—Lepidoptera
Family—Papilionidae
Genus—*Papilio*
Species—*glaucus*

The technical name of any plant or animal is made up of its genus and species. Thus, the technical or scientific name of the tiger swallowtail is *Papilio glaucus*. You will find that, in most scientific books and other technical publications, the scientific name is followed by a man's name or an abbreviation of it. This is the person who gave the species name to the animal or plant. Thus, the name of the tiger swallowtail is usually written *Papilio glaucus* Linn. This is because Linnaeus named it. The genus and species names are always in italics.

To understand how this system works in practice, let me recount an experience of my own. While a student in college I collected an unusual butterfly in the mountains of Montana. Realizing that this butterfly might be new to science, I sent specimens to an authority on butterflies, Dr. J. H. McDunnough. Dr. McDunnough determined that the butterfly was, indeed, a new species of the genus *Euphydryas* and named if after me. The technical name then became *Euphydryas hutchinsi* McD.

Insects belonging to the same family usually have similar life histories. That is, they pass through similar stages of growth and development.

All insects develop from eggs, and these are among the most interesting and attractive small objects in nature. They vary in size from microscopic to nearly a quarter of an inch in length. In general, the size of the eggs is related to the size of the insect that lays them, but there are many exceptions. The eggs of large dragonflies, for example, are quite small.

On the other hand, aphids or plant lice lay rather large eggs in proportion to their size.

There is also great variation in the shapes of insect eggs. Many are elongate, others are disk-like, conical, pyramidal, cylindrical, or vase-like. Grasshopper eggs are elongate, those of the giant walkingstick resemble tiny hand grenades. Butterfly eggs of most kinds have their outer walls sculptured in beautiful patterns. The eggs of harlequin cabbage bugs look like miniature kegs complete with hoops and bungs. Some eggs have a lid or *operculum* through which the young will eventually emerge. In the case of some shield bugs, this operculum is surrounded by a row of spines. Those of the poultry louse have hooks and spines, causing them to stick to feathers. Mayfly eggs have attached tendrils or filaments that become entangled in water plants, preventing them being carried away by currents. The eggs of katydids are disk-shaped.

Insects lay their eggs in all sorts of places. In general, they are laid on or near their food plants or in or upon animals that serve as hosts. Caddis insects drop their eggs in water where their larvae will live. The same is true of dragonflies. Walkingstick insects, living in trees, simply drop their eggs to the ground, leaving it to the young to crawl up into the trees to feed when spring arrives. Yet many insects take great care in placing their eggs upon the special food plants preferred by their young. I once sat beside a jungle trail watching a swallowtail butterfly laying her eggs. She would drop down and lay an egg upon a leaf, then flutter away and lay an egg on another leaf. Upon investigation I discovered that each time she laid an egg it was upon a wild citrus leaf. It was upon these shrubs, I knew, that her caterpillars fed. How, I wondered, did she identify the plants? Probably it was by their odor.

Many years ago I was engaged in studying the fly parasites of range grasshoppers in Montana. These flies darted at jumping grasshoppers, depositing their eggs upon the grasshoppers while in the air. I discovered that if a small, tightly rolled ball of paper was flipped through the air, one of the parasitic flies would dart at it, depositing one of her eggs upon it. In almost every case, an egg would be found attached to the ball of paper when I retrieved it.

The human bot fly (*Dermatobia hominus*) of the tropics uses another trick to assure that her eggs will hatch upon the skin of a human. The female attaches her eggs to certain mosquitoes (*Psorophora*). When such a mosquito bites a man the eggs hatch at once and the larval fly burrows into the skin. Flies of other kinds besides the mosquito may also serve as carriers of human bot fly eggs.

The methods used by insects to protect their eggs are almost endless. Some kinds insert their eggs into leaves or plant stems. Some are inserted into apples and other fruit. However, no matter how well an insect may protect its eggs and its young, some other insect will find a way to feed upon them or parasitize them. The horntail wasp (*Tremex*) inserts her eggs in the stems of woody plants where the young will later bore and feed. Here it would seem that the grubs would be safe from enemies. However, another wasp *(Megarhyssa lunator)* has a long *ovipositor* (egg-laying tube) by which she can bore into the solid wood in order to lay her egg in the horntail larva in which her young will live as a parasite, eventually killing it.

Most insect eggs hatch after being laid, but there are a number of insects in which the eggs hatch within the bodies of the female and, as a result, the young are born alive. These are known as *ovoviviparous* insects. Examples of this occur among aphids, certain flies, and some other insects.

There is great variation in the number of eggs laid by individual females. Aphids lay only a few. By contrast, queens of social insects such as ants, bees, and wasps may lay thousands.

A termite queen—another social insect—may lay more than a million eggs during her lifetime.

While both birds and insects begin life as eggs, their development from then on differs greatly. A bird grows up, gradually increasing in size as it matures and becomes an adult. By contrast, most insects pass through several definite steps or stages, each one differing from the previous one. A moth, for example, has four stages in its life history; egg, caterpillar (larva), pupa, and adult.

There are many variations in the life histories of insects but, in general, an insect grows, increasing in size by periodically shedding its outer hard covering or skin. Thus, a moth caterpillar grows larger by molting its skin a number of times. Each time it sheds its skin it becomes a little larger. This type of growth is necessary because an insect has an *exoskeleton*. That is, its outer hard shell serves as its skeleton. It has no bones, as in the case of a bird or a cat. An insect's muscles and organs are on the *inside* of its skeleton. Because of this, the insect must shed its outer hard covering if it is to grow larger.

The process of molting is known as *ecdysis*. The interval between molts is called a *stadium* (plural: *stadia*). The form of the insect during each stadium is called an *instar*. Thus, a tiny moth caterpillar just out of the egg is known as a first instar caterpillar. After shedding its skin for the first time it will be in its second instar, and so on. The number of molts varies, depending on the kind of insect. The changes through which an insect passes during its development is called its *life history* or *metamorphosis*.

There are several different types of life histories found in insects but authorities do not all agree as to their terminology. Some consider there to be only two types; others believe in dividing the life histories into many categories.

In this book, for simplicity, we will divide insect life histories into four types; primitive, gradual, incomplete, and complete. Brief summaries of the various types of life histories are:

PRIMITIVE LIFE HISTORIES—Simple development in which the young resemble the adults except for size. Found in the more primitive insects having no wings.

GRADUAL LIFE HISTORIES—Insects in which the young gradually change, step by step, until becoming adults. Most kinds are winged in the adult stage. The young are called *nymphs*.

INCOMPLETE LIFE HISTORIES—Insects in which the young develop and grow larger and, after becoming full grown, acquire wings without a pupal or resting stage. Most kinds live in the water during their immature stage. These young are called nymphs or, sometimes, *naiads*.

COMPLETE LIFE HISTORIES—In these insects there are four stages of development; egg, larva, pupa, and adult. In the pupal stage the insect is usually helpless and inactive. Most kinds are winged in the adult stage. Their young, or larvae, are usually caterpillars, grubs, or maggots.

Insects having primitive life histories are often classified as being *ametabolus,* meaning "without change." This is appropriate because there is, apparently, but little change during their growth from egg to adult, except for increase in size.

These insects are not often seen and are of minor importance from an economic standpoint. Still, they are of interest to the entomologist for a number of reasons. Their life histories furnish clues to the evolution of insects, and a few have unusual habits.

ORDER THYSANURA—SILVERFISH AND BRISTLETAILS

These insects trace their ancestry back to the lowest branch of the insect family tree. They were evolved before there were winged insects of any kind. They have chewing mouthparts and feed on a variety of foods. Some damage books or paper by feeding upon the starchy sizing. Others are scavengers, living in the soil, under stones, or beneath the bark of dead trees. Certain tiny species have taken up life in ant and termite nests, feeding upon debris found there. Some have eyes and some do not. Their bodies are slender and tapering, covered with fine scales or hairs. They run very rapidly or jump, and so are usually difficult to capture. One kind, usually called the firebrat (*Thermobia*), is tan in color and frequents warm places such as those near furnaces, fireplaces, or steam pipes.

Silverfish pass through no distinct stages of development. Newly hatched young look much like the adults except for size. This specimen is full grown. (Life size: 1/2 inch)

Collembola or springtails are tiny insects found in damp places. These congregated on the surface of a puddle. The young resemble the adults. (Life size: 1/16 inch)

ORDER COLLEMBOLA—SPRINGTAILS

To this order belong the springtails and snowfleas. They are very small in size, usually about one-sixteenth inch in length, and of little economic importance. However, they are of interest because of their structure and habits. Most kinds are able to jump five or six inches. This jumping ability is due to a forked structure, the spring or *furcula*, attached to their tails.

When preparing to jump, a springtail bends the furcula forward under its body where it is held in place by a catch or *tenaculum*. In jumping, the furcula snaps out of the tenaculum, causing the little insect to fly through the air. They often congregate upon the surface of water where they are able to use this jumping mechanism to propel themselves from the elastic surface film just as well as from a hard surface. To such small insects the water's surface film is like a tough membrane. This can be demonstrated by carefully laying a greasy needle upon the surface of a glass of water. The membrane-like surface film easily supports the steel needle.

Springtails are common in such moist places as among mosses, dead leaves, or in the soil. Some kinds inhabit caves; others live in the nests of termites or ants. Several kinds live upon beaches where they feed on organic matter deposited by the tides. Those living in termite and ant nests lack jumping organs. There are more than a thousand species of springtails in the world.

Perhaps the most interesting springtails are those known as snowfleas. There are several kinds and they occur in most parts of the world's cold regions. While young, these insects live in the soil. As adults, however, they often congregate upon the surface of the snow, especially during sunny days. In the mountains of the West I have often seen the snow covered with them. These groups would sometimes be a yard in diameter and, as I approached on skis, they would hop away, remaining together as a group. I was always amazed at finding such active insects in winter when most other insects were too cold to move.

The ones I saw in the mountains were probably the common snowflea (*Achorutes nivicolus*), found in most parts of the northern hemisphere. The golden snowflea (*Onychiurus cocklei*) is often found in large numbers on the surface of snow on the Pacific coasts from British Columbia to Alaska. Snowfleas are believed to feed upon pollen grains.

19

Part III: GRADUAL LIFE HISTORIES

Insects having gradual life histories pass through three stages of development; egg, nymph, and adult. The young insects, or nymphs, that hatch from the eggs resemble the adults except for size and the absence of fully-developed wings. The adults of some kinds never do acquire wings.

The term *nymph* is of Greek origin, meaning a "bride" or "maiden." In ancient mythology a nymph was a maiden who inhabited the mountains and forests.

As a rule, nymphs have the same food habits as the adults, being found upon the same food plants. Frequently they feed together.

In these insects there is no resting or inactive stage before the change into the winged adult.

ORDER ORTHOPTERA—GRASSHOPPERS AND THEIR RELATIVES

To this large and important group belong grasshoppers, crickets, katydids, roaches, mantises, and walkingsticks. Some of them are among the world's most destructive insect pests. Some are winged, while others are wingless. Many of them have *stridulating*, or singing, organs. There are several families.

FAMILY LOCUSTIDAE—THE GRASSHOPPERS

These insects begin life as eggs buried in the ground, and it is usually in this stage that winter is passed. In spring the eggs hatch and the young hoppers emerge from the ground and begin feeding. They have strong hind legs fitted for jumping, and mouthparts equipped for biting and chewing the plants upon which they feed. They are wingless. Even at this stage they may cause damage to crops and gardens if they are abundant.

These nymphal hoppers feed and grow rapidly and soon shed their outer skins to allow for increase in size. They usually molt about five times and after each molt they are larger in size. However, their body form does not change much. Short wings, or wing pads, appear at the time of the later molts. The larger these nymphs grow the more they eat, and so their destructive habits increase. Thus, it is during this period of growth that ranges and crops are often destroyed. In former years, before effective insecticides came into use, ranches and farms were helpless against the hoards of grasshoppers that devoured almost every green living thing. This was especially true in the West and Midwest.

At last, after the nymphs have become full grown, they shed their skins for the last time

Adult grasshoppers are winged, with hind legs fitted for jumping. Eggs are laid in the ground. (Life size: 1 inch)

21

and become adults. They now have fully-developed wings and are usually capable of flight. A few kinds, such as lubber grasshoppers (*Brachystola*), are too heavy-bodied to fly and their wings are very short.

As flying insects, they may travel long distances. In former years vast swarms of migratory grasshoppers (*Melanoplus spretus*), often called locusts, flew eastward from the Rocky Mountains and settled upon the range lands, causing tremendous damage in the Dakotas, Kansas, and Nebraska. Desert locusts (*Schistocerca*) fly in great swarms over Africa, Arabia, and other lands. Wherever they settle down, almost every bit of vegetation is destroyed and famines often result. This is true now, just as it was in Biblical times. Such migrating swarms have been seen more than a thousand miles at sea.

Near summer's end these winged grasshoppers mate, and the females lay their eggs in the ground. A female grasshopper inserts the tip of her abdomen in the ground and rotates her body, causing her abdomen to bore into the soil. Here, a mass of eggs is deposited, but they will not hatch until the following spring in our climate. Meanwhile, the adult grasshoppers all die, their mission in life completed.

Grasshopper eggs are elongate and deposited in the ground. These are from a lubber grasshopper. (Life size: 1/8 inch)

A young grasshopper or *nymph* looks very much like the adult except for its size and the absence of wings. (Life size: 1/2 inch)

This is an adult black cricket (*Gryllus*). It lays its eggs in the ground and the nymphs resemble the adults except that they are smaller and wingless. (Life size: 1 inch)

FAMILY GRYLLIDAE—THE CRICKETS

There are several types of crickets; some are ground-dwelling like the grasshoppers, while others live in trees and shrubs. The latter are usually called tree crickets. In general, the life histories of these insects are similar to those of grasshoppers. Adults are usually winged and the males often have sound-making organs. Most crickets are active at night.

Ground-inhabiting crickets deposit their eggs in the soil, using their spear-shaped *ovipositors*, or egg-laying tubes, for the purpose. Tree crickets insert their eggs in dead or living twigs.

Left: This adult bush katydid *(Microcentrum)* is green in color and is usually found in trees or shrubs. (Life size: 2 inches)

Above: Katydid eggs are laid on twigs and are disc-shaped. (Life size: 1/16 inch)

FAMILY TETTIGONIIDAE—THE KATYDIDS AND LONG-HORNED GRASSHOPPERS

These close relatives of the grasshoppers and.crickets have very long, thread-like antennae—the reason for the name, "long-horned"—and most kinds have well-developed sound-making organs. Some are called katydids because of the distinctive calls of the males. These kinds usually live in trees, but long-horned grasshoppers can be found in or among plants where their green coloration affords protection from enemies. A few are brown in color.

24

Eggs are usually attached to twigs or inserted into plant stems. Winter is most often passed in the egg stage, but a few kinds may over-winter as adults, especially in southern areas.

One of the more unusual of these insects is the large Mormon "cricket" (*Anabrus simplex*), a serious crop pest in certain areas of the West. In this case the adults are wingless. Eggs are laid in the ground and the young emerge in spring, and begin feeding upon local vegetation. Later, they may migrate in large droves across fields, destroying crops as they go. While they are called "crickets," they are actually more closely related to katydids.

Left: A young katydid resembles the adult. It is green and has very short wing pads. (Life size: 1/2 inch) Below: Long-horned grasshoppers are closely related to katydids. This is a tiny, nymphal long-horned grasshopper. (Life size: 1/4 inch)

This Carolina mantis *(Stagmomantis)* is green in color. Like all praying mantids, its forelegs are fitted for capturing prey. (Life size: 2 inches)

FAMILY MANTIDAE—THE MANTIDS

These are usually called praying mantids because they hold their front legs in an attitude of prayer. Actually, these legs are held in this position to enable the insect to reach out quickly and seize prey. This includes grasshoppers, flies, or other small insects.

In late summer the female deposits her eggs in clusters attached to small twigs. These egg clusters are covered with a hard coating that protects them from weather and enemies. Each cluster contains from twenty to forty eggs and the female may deposit several clusters. They over-winter in this stage.

The young mantids that hatch from the eggs the following spring are miniatures of the adults, but, of course, lack wings. Even at this stage of development they are hunters, capturing and feeding upon tiny insects such as aphids. They feed and grow, shedding their skins a number of times and changing their food items to larger and larger insects. They hide among leaves, grasping any insect so foolish as to stray too near.

By late summer they are ready to shed their skins for the last time and become winged adults. After mating, the females deposit their egg masses and die in the first frost. Thus does a mantis' year end, a life that is timed by the seasons.

Above: Mantids deposit their egg masses on twigs. Winter is passed in this stage. (Life size: 1 inch)

Right: Nymphal mantids are smaller than the adults and lack wings. Like the adults, they capture and feed upon other insects. (Life size: 1/2 inch)

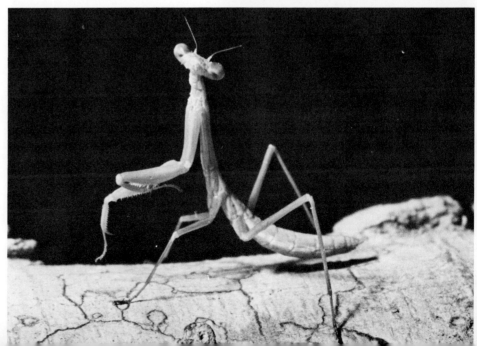

FAMILY PHASMIDAE—THE WALKINGSTICKS

These stick-shaped insects are especially abundant in warm and tropical lands. However, several kinds occur in the United States, but these are wingless. Some kinds found in tropical countries are winged and have green, leaf-like expansions on their legs. Because of their green coloration they are difficult to see among the tree leaves where they live and feed. In size the walkingsticks found in our country vary from an inch or so to the giant walkingstick (*Megaphasma dentricus*) found in southeastern United States. It is about six inches long. Phasmids are all slow-moving insects and not easily seen.

Walkingstick insects of the United States drop their eggs to the ground under the trees in which they live. Since these eggs resemble seeds, they are difficult to see among the dead leaves and litter. Winter is passed in this stage. With the arrival of spring the nymphal walkingsticks hatch and crawl up into the trees and begin feeding. In this stage they resemble the adults very closely, since the adults do not have wings. Nymphs and adults are, therefore, quite similar except for

This is a giant walkingstick insect *(Megaphasma)*, the largest insect found in the United States. It lives in trees and feeds on the leaves. (Life size: 6 inches)

size. As time passes, these nymphs continue to grow, molting their skins several times until the adult stage is reached in autumn. There is, thus, but one generation a year in our climate.

Right: Walkingstick insects in the act of mating. The male (bottom) is much smaller than the female. (Life size, female: 2 inches)

Below: Walkingstick eggs are dropped to the ground beneath the trees where the adults are feeding. It is in this stage that winter is passed. These are the eggs of the giant walkingstick. (Life size: 1/16 inch)

FAMILY BLATTIDAE—THE ROACHES

These are among the most common of all insects. They are found in every land except the Arctic and Antarctic, but are especially abundant in warm climates. Many kinds live in human habitations, but even more dwell in forests and jungles. Those that are pests in homes are usually brown, but tropical species range from bright green to red and other gay colors.

Roaches were abundant in the ancient forests when the coal beds were being formed and, thus, their ancestry reaches far back in time. Many roaches are winged and all of them can run swiftly to avoid capture. Their habits are nocturnal.

With regard to reproduction, roaches are said to be either *oviparous* or *ovoviviparous*. Oviparous roaches lay their eggs in leathery capsules called an *oötheca* (plural *oöthecae*). Often these capsules are carried about, attached to the abdomen of the female. Eventually they are dropped, usually in some sheltered location, and the young soon hatch. In the case of roaches that are ovoviviparous, the eggs are retained within the body of the female until they hatch. Thus, it may be said that these nymphs are born alive.

Young roaches, or nymphs, resemble the adults but are smaller. They are scavengers, feeding upon waste material and decaying plant and animal matter. The nymphs feed and grow, molting from five to seven times. Most kinds acquire wings. In general, roaches are long lived. While some pest species need only a few months to complete their life histories, other species require up to five years.

This adult, winged cockroach is from Panama. Like all roaches, this one is a scavenger. (Life size: 4 inches across)

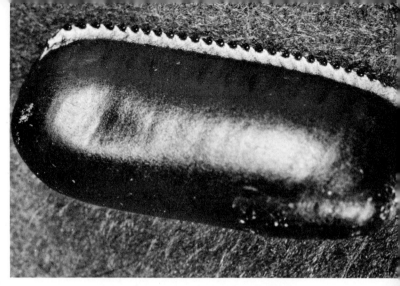

Close-up of a cockroach egg capsule. (Life size: 1/4 inch)

Cockroaches' eggs are laid in capsules containing many eggs. These capsules are carried about for several days, still attached to the female's abdomen. (Life size: 1/4 inch)

A roach nymph is shown in the process of shedding its outer skin. The newly emerged roach will darken in color in a few hours. (Life size: 1 inch)

ORDER ISOPTERA—TERMITES

Insects of this order are of small size, but of great economic importance. Most termites feed upon wood and are thus destructive to homes and other structures built of wood and wood products. They are sometimes called "white ants," but they are not even closely related to true ants. Termites are soft-bodied insects.

Termites are also highly specialized insects that live in colonies, often of large size. They live by a caste system. In a typical termite colony there are several different castes. First, there are the kings and queens, or reproductive males and females. These have dark bodies and possess eyes and wings in the adult stage. In some tropical species the queens may be very large; frequently three inches or more long and having their abdomens filled with eggs. The kings and queens are the only individuals that ever leave the colony. At certain

Left: Termite kings and queens are black and have wings. They are the only individuals to leave the colony. Also shown here, at left, is a worker. (Life size, king and queen: 1/2 inch) Center: A nymphal queen termite in a tunnel in wood. Note her short wings. (Life size 1/4 inch) Right: After mating, a termite queen severs her wings and devotes her energies to egg laying. Note her swollen abdomen filled with eggs. (Life size: 1/2 inch)

seasons they swarm out of the colony and mate. Later, they establish new colonies. At this time they shed their wings, since they will have no further use for them.

Unlike true ants, termites have a caste called *supplementary reproductives*. These individuals have very short wings and the females lay eggs, thus aiding the true queen in this task.

Most of the work of the colony is carried out by the worker caste. In a typical termite colony there are apt to be several thousand workers. They work at nest building and caring for young, as well as obtaining and digesting food. These are the usual individuals seen when a dead log or stump is broken open. Workers are white-bodied and wingless. Unlike true ant workers, which are all females, termite workers may be of either sex. While these typical, wingless workers are found in most kinds of the termites dwelling in North America, some tropical species have no true worker caste. In this case, the work of the colony is carried out by the nymphs. Perhaps this is a case of "child labor."

In most termite colonies yet another caste is present. These are the soldiers whose duty is the protection of the colony. They are somewhat larger than the workers and have enlarged heads and large jaws. They may be of either sex. Often, when danger threatens, the soldiers sound the alarm by tapping their heads and jaws upon the passages of the colony. These sounds can frequently be heard by the human ear.

Usually termites inhabit damp situations or live in the ground. Most unusual is their ability to digest the hard cellulose of wood. Most of the species found in the United States dwell underground or in wood, but in some tropical countries they construct nests rising thirty feet above the level of the earth. Some of these termites have the habit of cultivating and feeding upon fungi which they grow in their nests.

Perhaps the most unusual termites are the so-called magnetic termites of Australia that construct wedge-shaped mounds rising as high as twelve feet above the level of the land. The interesting thing is that these mounds always have their narrow ends facing north and south, the reason they are called "magnetic."

ORDER HEMIPTERA—HALF-WINGED BUGS

To this large and important order belong true bugs of many kinds. The term "bug" should properly only be applied to these insects and those of the order Homoptera. Most bugs have wings, but the wings of the Hemiptera are of special form. The basal portions of the front wings are thickened and leathery, while the apical portions are membranous. This is the reason for the name of the order. Hempitera is a Greek term meaning "half-wings." The thin hind wings are usually folded under the front wings when the insects are at rest. Their mouthparts are fitted for piercing and sucking, and most kinds live upon plant juices and sap. A few are blood-suckers.

The young, called nymphs, are usually similar in appearance to the adults, except that they have no wings and are smaller. After hatching from the egg, a bug molts half a dozen times and at the last molt, fully-developed wings appear.

This order contains many families, but space permits the inclusion of only a few of the more important ones.

34

FAMILY PENTATOMIDAE—THE STINK BUGS

The family name of these insects is of Greek origin, meaning "five-cut," in reference to the five joints of their antennae. They are usually oval in form and feed upon plant sap. A few capture and feed upon other insects. The nymphs have scent glands on the tops of their abdomens that secrete an ill-smelling substance. After changing into the adult stage, similar glands occur on the sides of the thorax.

These bugs are usually green, brown, or black, and about half an inch long. Some tropical species, however, are much larger and are frequently arrayed in gay colors and bright markings. The nymphs resemble the adults.

One of the most common members of this family is the harlequin cabbage bug *(Murgantia histrionica)*, a serious pest of cabbage and related plants. It is a pretty insect marked with black and red. Its eggs are especially interesting when viewed under a lens. They are laid in groups and resemble tiny barrels complete with hoops and bungs. All stages—eggs, nymphs, and adults—may often be found on cabbages in southeastern United States.

Stink bugs have five-segmented antennae and glands that produce ill-smelling odors. This is an adult with well-developed wings. (Life size 1/2 inch)

35

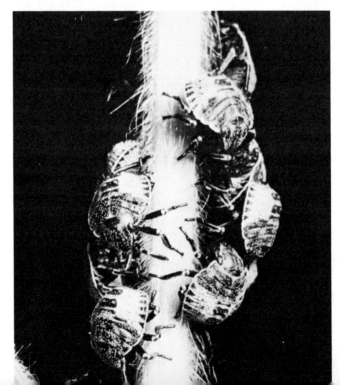

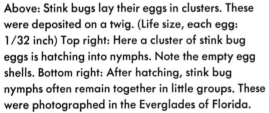

Above: Stink bugs lay their eggs in clusters. These were deposited on a twig. (Life size, each egg: 1/32 inch) Top right: Here a cluster of stink bug eggs is hatching into nymphs. Note the empty egg shells. Bottom right: After hatching, stink bug nymphs often remain together in little groups. These were photographed in the Everglades of Florida.

Above: The eggs of the harlequin cabbage bug resemble tiny barrels complete with hoops and bungs. (Life size, each egg: 1/16 inch)

Left: The harlequin cabbage bug has red and black markings. It is a serious pest of plants of the mustard family. (Life size: 1/2 inch)

FAMILY COREIDAE—THE SQUASH BUGS AND LEAF-LEGGED BUGS

These bugs have elongate bodies and vary in size from tiny to nearly an inch in length. Most of our species are brown or other dull colors, but many tropical kinds are dressed in bright hues. In most cases their legs are of the usual form, but some have leaf-like enlargements or expansions from which the name "leaf-legged" bugs is derived. Most kinds feed upon plants, and some kinds are harmful pests. The nymphs are similar to the adults and have similar habits.

Common coreids include the leaf-legged bug *(Leptoglossus)* and the common sqaush bug *(Anasa)*.

A squash bug in the act of laying her eggs on a squash leaf. (Life size: 1/2 inch)

Close-up of squash bug eggs. (Life size: 1/16 inch)

Closely related to squash bugs are the leaf-legged bugs *(Leptoglossus)*, with leaf-like expansions on their hind legs. This is an adult. The nymphs have short wings. (Life size: 3/4 inch)

Wheel bugs *(Arilus)* belong to the assassin bug family. They and their nymphs capture and suck the blood of other insects. (Life size: 1 inch)

Opposite left: Wheel bugs lay their eggs in clusters attached to plants. (Life size of cluster: 1/4 inch)

Top right: Assassin bug nymphs hatching from an egg cluster.

Bottom: Assassin bug nymph. Note the absence of wings in this stage. Like the adult, it feeds upon other insects. (Life size: 1/4 inch)

FAMILY REDUVIIDAE—THE ASSASSIN BUGS AND WHEEL BUGS

These small-to-large bugs have somewhat flattened bodies and, like the ambush bugs, hide in plants or flowers waiting for insect prey. Their colors vary from black to bright hues of red and orange. Some kinds are considered to be beneficial to man, since they capture bedbugs and other household pests. One kind is the kissing bug *(Triatoma sanguisuga)* that may inflict severe wounds on man. It has been known to bite the lips. A tropical species carries deadly Chagas' disease of humans. Adults and nymphs have similar habits.

An easily recognized member of this family is the wheel bug *(Arilus cristatus)*, characterized by having a cogwheel-like crest on its back. Both adults and nymphs feed upon other insects. The adults are nearly black but the nymphs are blood-red with black markings. The nymphs lack the cogwheel ornamentation on their backs.

FAMILY NEPIDAE—THE WATER SCORPIONS

These unusual insects live in the water where they prey upon other water insects. They have elongate bodies and their front legs are fitted for capturing their prey. They usually hide in aquatic vegetation waiting for their game to approach. Extending out of their tails are slender breathing tubes which they push up above the water's surface to obtain air. They have well-developed wings and sometimes leave the water and fly about.

These peculiar insects insert their eggs in rotting wood or attach them to objects in the water. Their eggs are easily recognized; attached to each one are several slender filaments. The nymphs have habits quite similar to those of the adults.

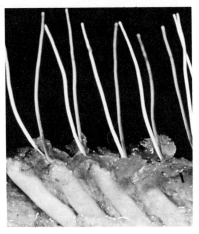

Top: Water scorpions live in water, breathing by means of a long snorkle pushed above the surface. They eat other water insects, in this case a dragonfly nymph. (Life size: 3 inches)

Bottom: Water scorpions insert their eggs in submerged rotting wood. Each egg has two breathing filaments attached to it. (Life size, each egg: 1/16 inch)

FAMILY BELOSTOMATIDAE—
THE GIANT WATER BUGS

These bugs have flattened bodies and are of large size, some as long as four inches. They are the largest of all bugs.

Their front legs are fitted for grasping prey and they are able to inject a powerful venom into any creature they capture. Their prey consists of small fish, tadpoles, frogs, and small snakes. They also capture other aquatic insects.

These large bugs have wings and frequently fly to lights at night, and it is for this reason that they are sometimes known as "electric light" bugs.

There are several species, some of which attach their eggs to underwater objects. Other kinds glue their eggs to the backs of the males, who are thus forced to protect them until they hatch. Like the adults, the nymphs are predaceous, but their prey is of smaller size. The nymphs resemble the adults except that they have shorter wings.

Giant water bugs dwell in ponds and streams, but sometimes leave the water and fly about. The female (top) lays her eggs on the back of the male and he is forced to guard them until they hatch into nymphs. (Life size: 2 inches)

43

FAMILIES NOTONECTIDAE AND CORIXIDAE—THE BACKSWIMMERS AND WATER BOATMEN

There are two kinds of small bugs often seen darting about in the water. Both kinds are shaped like miniature submarines. However, the backswimmers swim on their backs, while those of the other family (Corixidae) swim in the usual manner, darting about, propelled by their long, oar-like legs.

The family name of the backswimmers (Notonectidae) is of Greek origin, meaning "swimming on the back." They are common in ponds and small streams where they feed upon small water insects, captured by means of their front legs.

These insert their eggs into water plants or glue them to underwater objects. The nymphs resemble the adults except for undeveloped wings and their smaller size. They have similar habits. Winter is passed in both nymphal and adult stages. The winged adults frequently leave the water and fly to lights. While under water they carry supplies of air on the surfaces of their bodies and under their wings. This air coating gives them a silvery appearance.

The hind legs of water boatmen and backswimmers are long and oar-like, used to propel them through the water. Water boatmen swim with their backs uppermost; backswimmers swim on their backs. The nymphs of both kinds have short wings. This is a water boatman. (Life size: 1/2 inch)

ORDER HOMOPTERA—CLEAR-WINGED BUGS

Classified in this large and important group are insects having various habits and characteristics. Unlike the members of the order Hemiptera (half-winged bugs), the wings of these insects, when present, are of uniform thickness and texture throughout. The name of the order—Homoptera—is of Greek origin, meaning "same winged."

Some of these bugs have very complex life histories. All have mouthparts fitted for sucking out the sap of plants. For this reason some kinds are serious pests.

All these insects have three stages in their life histories; egg, nymph, and winged adult. Some, however, never do acquire wings. The nymphs look much like the adults.

FAMILY CICADIDAE—THE CICADAS

These are the largest of the bugs belonging to this order. They vary in size from half an inch in length to nearly two inches. Most native species are about an inch and a half long and have wingspreads of nearly two inches.

Sometimes called "harvest flies," they live in the ground as nymphs for long periods, then emerge, acquire wings, mate, and lay their eggs. One kind, the famous seventeen-year locust or periodical cicada (*Magicicada septendecim*), lives in the ground as a nymph for seventeen years. During this time its food consists of sap siphoned from tree roots. During the seventeenth summer the nymphs burrow upward through the soil and eventually emerge. Once above the ground's surface, they crawl up the trunks of trees and shed their skins for the last time, becoming winged cicadas. Their old, discarded nymphal skins are left clinging to the bark. Often these cicadas emerge in such tremendous numbers that the forests ring with their songs. Only the males have sound-making organs. These consist of drumming mechanisms, the drums being activated by muscles on their inside surfaces.

Mating eventually occurs and the females then lay their eggs in twigs. These eggs are inserted into the twigs by the females' sharp ovipositors, or egg-laying tubes. Within a few days the eggs hatch and the tiny, ant-like nymphs drop to the ground and burrow in. As time passes, they burrow deeper and deeper into the ground, eventually reaching a depth of about three feet. As the years pass, they feed during the summers and remain inactive

Left: Adult cicadas insert their eggs in living twigs, using their spear-like ovipositors for the purpose. (Life size: 2 inches) Right: Here a twig containing cicada eggs has been split open to reveal them. The eggs will soon hatch and the tiny nymphs will drop to the ground. (Life size: 1/16 inch)

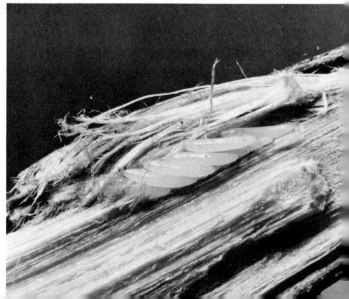

Left: A cicada nymph in the act of hatching from an egg inserted in a twig by a female cicada. It will drop to the ground and burrow in. (Life size: 1/16 inch) Right: After many years in the ground the cicada nymph emerges, a slit opens down its back and the adult cicada appears. At first it is white, but its wings slowly expand and harden. Note the nymphal skin left clinging to the bark of the tree. (Life size of adult: 1 inch)

during the winters. However, when the seventeenth summer arrives they cease feeding, tunnel up to the surface, and the life cycle starts over again. Various groups, or *broods*, occur in different localities. Thus, these cicadas may be very abundant in some area each summer.

The seventeen-year cicadas are found in northeastern United States, but a similar species occurs in the Southeast. The latter species requires only thirteen years to complete its life history.

The above is a brief summary of the life history of the periodical cicadas, but there are numerous other cicadas found in various parts of North America. These spend only two or three years in the ground. They are usually present each summer.

47

Treehoppers are often of peculiar form and some are quite colorful. This adult lives on oak. (Life size: 1/4 inch)

Like the adults, nymphal treehoppers siphon out the sap of trees. Their wings are short. (Life size: 1/4 inch)

FAMILY MEMBRACIDAE—THE TREEHOPPERS

Treehoppers have their *pronotums* (segment back of the head) extended forward over the head and backward over the abdomen. Some species, especially those found in tropical regions, have the pronotum decorated with spines or horns. Most treehoppers are about a quarter of an inch long.

They are usually found living in trees and shrubs, and lay their eggs in the bark. The nymphs of some species feed upon grasses and weeds; later, as winged adults, they migrate to trees. Winter is usually passed in the egg stage.

FAMILY CERCOPIDAE—THE FROGHOPPERS OR SPITTLE BUGS

These are small insects, rarely over half an inch long. As nymphs they live in masses of foam upon grasses and weeds. This frothy material no doubt has a protective function. Their habit of secreting these masses of froth is the reason that they are usually called "spittle bugs."

After molting for the last time and becoming adults, they leave the protective masses of foam and move or fly about. They lay their eggs in the stems of the plants where their nymphs will feed.

Left: Froghopper adults are winged and suck out the sap of plants. This one is red and black. (Life size: 1/4 inch) Center: Froghopper nymphs protect themselves in foam-like masses of froth. They live inside, siphoning out the sap of the plant. (Life size: 1/2 inch) Right: Here a froghopper nymph has been exposed by removing its froth-like covering. (Life size: 1/4 inch)

Leafhoppers live upon plants, sucking out sap with their sharp beaks. The nymphs are similar but have short wings. (Life size: 1/8 inch)

FAMILY CICADELLIDAE—THE LEAFHOPPERS

These are small insects that look like miniature cicadas. They vary in size, but are rarely as long as half an inch. Most kinds measure about half that size. Many of them are highly colored.

Leafhoppers feed upon almost all kinds of plants and trees, depending on the species. Some are of great economic importance because. they carry serious plant diseases. They are common insects and there are numerous species.

Winter is usually passed in the egg stage, but a few kinds over-winter as adults. The eggs are inserted in the stems of plants. After four or five molts, the nymphs become winged adults. There may be several complete generations a summer.

FAMILY APHIDIDAE—THE APHIDS OR PLANT LICE

Aphids are tiny insects which are found almost everywhere and, frequently, cause great damage to the plants upon which they live and feed.

They are soft-bodied, and usually green in color. Attached to their abdomens are two tube-like structures called *cornicles*. From these cornicles is secreted honeydew, which is actually excess sweetish sap sucked from the plants upon which they feed by means of their piercing beaks.

Many aphids have very complicated life histories. Most kinds over-winter in the egg stage. In spring these eggs hatch into nymphs that develop into wingless females that give birth to living young without mating. Several generations may be produced in this way, all from unmated females. Eventually winged females are produced and, often, these fly to another

Aphids live upon plants and suck out the sap. Shown here is a winged adult and two nymphs. (Life size: 1/8 inch)

kind of plant where they continue to reproduce. Later, they fly back to the original host plant where the nymphs develop into winged males and females. After mating, the adult females lay the eggs that over-winter.

Not all aphids follow this type of life history. Some remain on the same plant all summer, where large colonies arise. The woolly alder aphid (*Prociphalus tessellatus*) secretes masses of white wax. A similar aphid (*Eriosoma lanigerum*) lives on apple. It is known as the woolly apple aphid.

Left: This aphid is also an adult but it has no wings. Note the two *cornicles* at the rear end of its body. (Life size: 1/8

inch) Right: Shown here is a wingless adult aphid in the act of laying an egg. (Life size: 1/8 inch)

Part IV: INCOMPLETE LIFE HISTORIES

Long ago, certain insects took up life in the water, that is, they became aquatic in habits, especially during their immature or nymphal stages. The adults, however, were winged and lived in the air or near the water. In order to make the sudden change from an aquatic nymph to an adult fitted for aerial life, a special type of life history was evolved. This did not include a pupal or inactive resting stage, which was an advantage because pupae are unable to defend themselves and so may be destroyed by enemies. In these insects, there are only three stages of development; egg, nymph, and adult. These are the same stages found in insects having a gradual life history, the chief difference being that the change from nymph to winged adult is more abrupt, both in habits and in appearance. These young aquatic insects are sometimes called *naiads*.

The abrupt change that these insects pass through from water-living nymphs to air-living adults is one of Nature's miracles. It is almost as if a submarine could suddenly sprout wings and fly. This would, indeed, be a remarkable feat, yet it is one that these insects have been doing for millions of years.

ORDER PLECOPTERA—STONEFLIES

These insects are of medium-to-large size and have flattened bodies. The adults are winged and, when at rest, fold their wings fan-like over their backs. The adults are often abundant at certain seasons and are sometimes called salmonflies.

Adult stoneflies vary in size. This is a large stonefly from the Great Smoky Mountains. Note the folded wings. (Life size: 2 inches)

Stonefly nymphs, or naiads, live in the water. Notice the unusual markings and the feather-like gills along the sides of the body. (Life size: 1 inch)

Female stoneflies lay their eggs in the water, often as many as 6,000. Upon hatching, the tiny nymphs or naiads live underwater. They are especially abundant in clear mountain streams where they may be found creeping over the under surfaces of rocks or dead limbs. Close examination reveals tufts or gills along each side of their abdomens. It is by means of these gills that the nymphs obtain oxygen from the water. Some kinds have gills at the rear end of the body. Most species feed upon small aquatic insects, others eat algae.

After a number of molts, the nymphs may reach a length of nearly two inches, depending on the species. When ready to transform into an adult, a nymph crawls out of the water, usually up the side of an exposed stone or the stem of a willow, and a slit soon opens down its back. The adult insect then crawls out of its nymphal skin and, when its wings expand

and harden, it flies away. Its old skin is left clinging to the site where it transformed.

Stoneflies are of interest to fishermen, since they constitute important fish food items, both as nymphs and as adults. The time when the adults are emerging is usually the best time to catch trout in mountain streams.

ORDER ODONATA—DRAGONFLIES AND DAMSELFLIES

These are the most remarkable of all flying insects. No other creature can match their flying ability. The adults dart over ponds and streams, capturing the insects upon which they prey. Some kinds are very colorful, and are almost as attractive as butterflies. They vary in size from one to six inches across. They feed upon gnats, mosquitoes, or other small insects. Damselflies, when at rest, fold their wings over their backs, but dragonflies do not. As a rule, damselflies are smaller and less robust than dragonflies. Otherwise, they are similar both in appearance and in habits.

Dragonflies are among the world's most efficient fliers. This adult rests on a weed near a pond. (Life size: 3 inches)

55

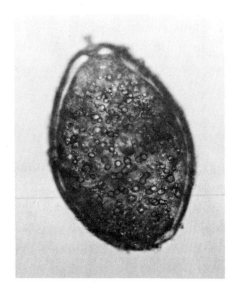

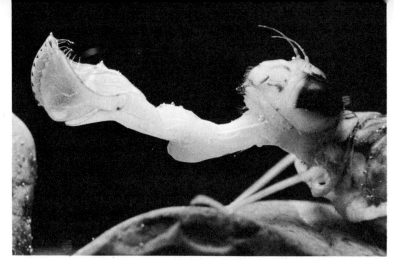

Left: A dragonfly egg. Dragonflies lay their eggs in the water where their nymphs, or naiads, will live. (Life size: 1/64 inch) Right: Dragonfly nymphs live in the water where they capture their prey by means of "lip-traps." This photograph shows how the nymph's lower lip is modified into an organ that may be thrust out to seize prey. Note the toothed jaws at its tip. (Life size, nymph: 1 inch)

It is not unusual to see a dragonfly darting about over a pond, dropping down now and then to touch the water's surface with the tip of its abdomen or tail. Each time it touches the water's surface it lays an egg. Dragonflies of many kinds push their abdomens down under the water and lay their eggs in masses. Sometimes these masses may contain nearly a thousand eggs. The eggs settle to the bottom and hatch into tiny nymphs or naiads which feed upon small items of aquatic life.

The nymphs continue to feed and grow, molting their skins ten or fifteen times over a period of from one to five years, depending on the species. During this time they live on the bottoms of ponds, brooks, or streams or hide just beneath the sand or mud. A dragonfly nymph's method of capturing its prey is unique among animals. Its lower lip is modified into a mechanism having jaws at its tip. This "lip-trap" can be thrust out for some distance to seize prey. Mostly, these nymphs "play a waiting game," hiding among water plants or under the sand or mud at the bottom. When any unwary insect approaches, the nymph flips out its liptrap and grabs it.

In addition to its unique prey-capturing mechanism, many dragonfly nymphs use an unusual means of swimming. When alarmed, the nymph sucks water into the rectal cavity at the tip of its abdomen and then ejects this water under pressure. As a result, the insect's body is thrust forward at considerable speed. Thus, it swims by jet propulsion. This can easily

Left: Here an adult dragonfly emerges from its nymphal skin. At this time its body is white and soft. (Life size: 3 inches) See next photograph.

Right: After an hour or so, the wings expand and harden. It is now about ready for flight. Notice the nymphal skin still clinging to the grass stem.

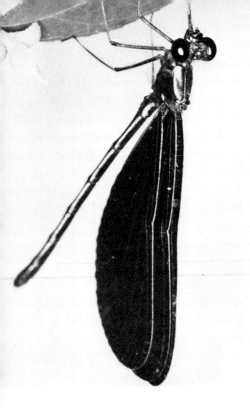

be observed by watching one of the nymphs in an aquarium. It will also be noticed that its movement through the water is not steady; instead, it thrusts itself along in a "jerky" fashion. This results from the alternate filling and ejection of water from its rectal cavity.

At the end of the nymph's underwater life, when it is full grown, it creeps toward the shore or bank and climbs up the stem of some plant. This usually occurs at night. A foot or so above the water's surface, the nymph anchors its feet in the bark and rests quietly. Soon a seam opens down its back and the adult, winged dragonfly or damselfly, crawls out of the nymphal skin. The wings are at first crumpled and soft, but they soon expand and harden, and the insect is then ready to dart over the surrounding area capturing prey. The ugly nymph has been quickly transformed into a sleek, alert, winged insect, probably the most skillful flying creature the world has ever known.

Above: Damselflies are close relatives of dragonflies. This black damselfly perches on a leaf. (Life size: wingspread, 2 inches across)

Right: Damselfly nymphs have three tail-like gills for obtaining oxygen from the water. This nymph is almost ready to transform into an adult. Note the four wing pads. (Life size: 1 inch)

Part V: COMPLETE LIFE HISTORIES

In their long evolutionary history insects have followed a complicated path. Any insect or insect group that has survived to the present has done so because it was well adapted to its environment and able to change as its environment slowly changed. Down the millions of years of their existence they have had to cope with tremendous alterations in their surroundings. There have been long periods when the world's climates were cold, when frigid Ice Age snows moved southward and northward from the poles. Volcanoes have erupted, pouring poisonous gases into the air and covering the land with ash. The continents themselves have gradually moved across the face of the earth, altering forever world topography. Mountains have been thrust up from level plains and then submerged beneath the sea, only to be pushed upward again. New enemies and diseases have added hazards to life. In spite of all these difficulties, insects have survived and flourished.

From the standpoint of evolutionary development, those insects highest on the family tree are the ones having complete life histories, that is, those insects that pass through four steps or stages of development: egg, larva, pupa, and adult. Most of these insects are winged in the adult stage. The possession of wings is a definite sign of evolutionary superiority. The ability to fly is a major step in the history of any creature, including man.

Among these insects the young that hatch from the eggs are called *larvae* (singular: *larva*). They are usually in the form of a caterpillar, a grub, or a maggot. Caterpillars are elongate and soft-bodied, and creep about on their legs. They are of various colors and sizes and are familiar to almost everyone. Grubs are usually white, the most common kinds living in the soil. Their bodies are most often curled up in the form of a C. They have well-developed legs and chewing mouthparts. Maggots, by contrast, are spindle-shaped and have no legs. They are white in color and their mouthparts are inconspicuous. However, since these larvae vary in form, they are often known by different common names. A few examples:

Geometrid moth larvae—loopers or measuringworms
Psychid moth larvae—bagworms
Mosquito larvae—wigglers or wrigglers
Mymeleonid larvae—ant lions
Chrysopid larvae—aphis lions
Moth caterpillars that roll themselves in leaves—leaf-rollers
Caterpillars that build cases around themselves—casebearers
Eucleid moth larvae—slug caterpillars
Elaterid beetle larvae—wireworms
May and June beetle larvae—white grubs

It should be noted that the term "worm" should not properly be applied to insect young, even though this is often done. This term should technically be used only for such creatures as earthworms, hair worms, and so on. True worms are not even closely related to insects.

Most insect larvae have jaws and feed upon plants or animals, but there are many exceptions.

Fly larvae (maggots), for example, do not possess true jaws. Most larvae have legs, but some are legless, as in the case of larval flies, bees, wasps, and ants.

One characteristic of many larvae, especially those of moths, is the ability to produce silk. This useful substance is the product of large glands located in the body cavity. Ducts carry the liquid silk to openings called *spinnerets* located in the *labium* (lower lip). As the silk issues from the spinnerets it hardens into thin thread-like strands. It is this material that the larva uses in spinning its cocoon. It is very tough and so affords protection to the pupal insect within. This is also the silk obtained from commercial silk worms, which are the larvae of moths, and used in the spinning of silken garments.

Insect larvae vary greatly in form. Those of butterflies and moths are typical caterpillars and crawl about, usually feeding upon plants. Others, including those of many beetles, are white and grub-like. They do not actively crawl about. Many beetle larvae, by contrast, are entirely different. Ground beetle larvae are of slender form, dark in color, and run actively about, searching for the insect prey upon which they feed.

The larvae of most flies are maggot-like and legless. Thus, they are wormlike. The technical word is *vermiform*, meaning "of worm form."

In general, the form of a larval insect is governed by the kind of life it leads. Larval honeybees, for example, develop in wax cells where they are well protected and fed by worker bees. These larvae have no need for legs, since they do not move about. A similar condition is found among the larvae of wasps, hornets, and ants.

It is during its larval stage that an insect does most of its feeding and growing. Thus, insect pests are usually most destructive during this stage. As a larval insect grows, it molts its skin several times to allow for increase in size. The number of molts varies with the insect. Some, such as moth caterpillars, molt about half a dozen times, but some others have many more molts.

Most insect larvae complete their growth in one summer or, often, in a few weeks. However, a few remain in this larval stage for several years, remaining inactive during winter and feeding again each summer. Probably the insect spending the longest period as a larva is that of a wood-boring beetle (family Cerambycidae). Adults of these beetles have emerged from furniture twenty years after manufacture. The parent beetles had evidently laid their eggs in the trees from which the furniture had been manufactured.

Having completed its growth, a larval insect becomes inactive and sheds its skin for the last time, changing into a *pupa* (plural: *pupae*). Usually, before changing into this stage, the larva seeks a protected place or constructs some sort of shelter. Moth caterpillars, in most cases, spin silken cocoons around themselves. However, other moth caterpillars roll themselves in leaves or burrow into the ground. Cutworms (a type of caterpillar) have the latter habit.

The pupa itself usually has a mummy-like appearance, but there are exceptions, as in many beetle pupae. The term *pupa* comes from Latin, a word meaning girl, doll, or puppet. It was first applied to butterfly pupae, now usually called *chrysalids*.

During the pupal stage, an insect does not feed and it is usually inactive. While in this stage, great changes take place in its body and internal organs. In the case of a butterfly or a moth, their habits change from feeding upon plant tissues to sucking out the nectar of flowers. The greatest change, however, is from a creeping caterpillar into a winged insect adapted for flight. In the process most of the sense organs are altered and the muscles converted into different ones that will power the wings. I am reminded of a recent cartoon in which a caterpillar, looking up at a butterfly, remarks, "You will never get me up in one of those things!" However, a caterpillar regularly performs this remarkable feat each time it changes itself into a pupa and then into a butterfly or a moth.

The changes that occur during an insect's pupal stage have been studied in some detail. First, there is a degeneration of most of the larval organs. This tearing down of the tissues is called *histolysis*. The next step is the rebuilding of new tissues and this is called *histogenesis*. There is considerable variation among insects as to the degree in which the larval organs are broken down. In many, the contents of the pupal case become semi-liquid. In the pupae of flies, all the internal organs are broken down except the central nervous system, the heart and the reproductive organs.

In some pupae the future legs and wings are visible on the outer surface, usually being pressed tightly against the outer pupal wall. In other cases these appendages are entirely free. In many pupae, however, there is no visible evidence of the future legs and wings. This is true of flies.

The types of pupae are classified on the visible presence or absence of future legs and wings. If the appendages are free, that is, not attached to the exterior of the pupal case, they are said to be *exarate*. If, however, they are closely pressed against the pupa's body wall, they are called *obtect* pupae. On the other hand, if the future appendages are not visible at all, they are said to be *coarctate*. This type is usually called a *puparium*. A few examples are:

Exarate pupae—nerve-winged insects, caddis insects, most beetles, and a few moths
Obtect pupae—most butterflies and moths, many beetles, and some flies
Coarctate pupae—most flies and a few other insects

While most pupae are inactive, a good many are capable of considerable movement. Mosquito pupae, often called "tumblers," are very active and quickly move deep into water when danger threatens. While almost any pupa will move slightly when disturbed, a few

This is the *exarate* pupa of a mud dauber wasp. In this case the legs and wings are free from the body. It is a pale ghost of the future wasp. (Life size: 1 inch)

This is the *obtect* pupa of a moth. The future legs and wings are closely pressed to the body. (Life size: 1 inch)

This is the *coarctate* pupa of a housefly. There is no visible evidence of the future legs or wings. (Life size: 1/4 inch)

kinds engage in active movements just before they are ready to change into adults. Sphinx caterpillars pupate in the soil and remain there. However, shortly before emerging as adults, they wriggle their way upward to near the ground's surface. Carpenter-worm caterpillars bore into solid wood and pupate in the tunnels. Before changing into adults they work their way to a point near the surface of the wood. Here the adult moths have little difficulty in freeing themselves.

Since many adult insects do not have jaws, the larvae, before changing into pupae, must make some kind of provision for the escape of the future adult. This is especially true of moth caterpillars that pupate in protective cocoons or inside plants. The silken cocoon of the cecropia moth is so constructed that there is a valve-like structure at one end. When the moth is ready to emerge it has merely to push out. Since it has no mouthparts capable of cutting through the silken wall of the cocoon, it would otherwise be unable to escape. The saddleback caterpillar fashions a lid-like structure at the upper end of its cocoon and the adult has only to push open the lid when it changes into the adult stage. Certain caterpillars live and feed inside the stems of goldenrod plants, causing the stems to enlarge into "galls." The adult moths will not emerge until the following spring, by which time the stems of the plants have become very hard and dry. Thus, these caterpillars must prepare an escape hatch. This they do by cutting an escape tunnel reaching almost to the outer surface of the gall-like swelling. The same technique is employed by the caterpillar that lives and feeds inside the Mexican jumping bean, the caterpillar that causes the bean to jump. Before pupating, the caterpillar cuts a neat opening through the wall. This opening is not cut completely through; just enough tissue is left to hold the door in place. Thus, when the moth emerges from its pupal case, it has merely to push open the lid and leave the bean.

Numerous other examples could be sighted to illustrate the remarkable "foresight" shown by many larvae. They indicate how well insects are adapted to the lives they live. Each larvae must, in some way, make provision for its future.

ORDER COLEOPTERA—BEETLES

This is the largest order of insects, more than a quarter of a million species having been cataloged in the world. In the United States, alone, there are over 25,000 kinds. They occur in almost every situation and feed upon almost every type of edible food. At least one kind—a beaver parasite—lives a parasitic existence.

Beetles vary in size from minute to over four inches long. Some are brilliantly colored. They are characterized by having four wings, the front pair hard and shield-like, covering the membranous hind wings which are folded beneath them. These front wings are called *elytra* (singular: *elytron*). It is from the hard, sheath-like nature of the front wings that the name of the order is derived. Coleoptera is a term of Greek origin meaning "sheath-wings."

Beetles have chewing mouthparts consisting of powerful jaws, capable, in many cases, of cutting through extremely hard substances. One kind of beetle causes damage to telephone lines by cutting through the lead sheathing of telephone cables.

The forewings of beetles are hard and shield-like. The membranous hind wings are folded beneath them. Here is shown a giant rhinoceros beetle in flight. (Life size: 2 inches)

67

Left: These are the eggs of a leaf beetle. They are typical beetle eggs. (Life size: 1/32 inch) Right: Most beetles have powerful jaws. Some beetles are able to cut through wood and other hard substances. These are the jaws of a tiger beetle, used to capture insect prey. (Life size: 1/8 inch)

All beetles have complete life histories consisting of egg, larva, pupa, and adult. The larvae vary greatly in form and habits. Many are grub-like. There are many families of beetles, but the following are probably the most important.

FAMILY CICINDELIDAE—THE TIGER BEETLES

The adults of this family are brightly colored in many cases, and very active, capturing and feeding upon other insects. They run rapidly upon the ground and are expert flyers. Most kinds are about half an inch long.

Larval tiger beetles have most interesting habits. They excavate vertical burrows in the ground, usually in dry paths, and hide inside them. These burrows are about the size of a pencil. The larvae have elongate bodies and large jaws, and wait in the entrances to their burrows with only their heads and jaws exposed. If any insect strays too near, the beetle larva reaches out and grabs it. The prey is then dragged down to the bottom of the burrow and devoured.

One of these tiger beetle larvae will not hesitate to seize an insect much larger than itself. In this case the tiger beetle larva might be dragged from its protective burrow were it not for a pair of hook-like spines on its back that anchor it securely inside.

Below: Tiger beetles are excellent fliers and also run very rapidly on the ground. They have keen eyesight. (Life size: 3/4 inch)

Right: Larval tiger beetles hide in holes in the ground with only their heads exposed. They capture insects that walk by. (Life size: 1 inch long)

FAMILY CARABIDAE—THE GROUND BEETLES

These are the black beetles frequently seen under boards or rocks. Usually half an inch or more in length, they run very rapidly and live chiefly upon caterpillars. In most cases they are black, but a few are reddish or have metallic coloration.

One kind, of special interest, is the bombardier beetle (*Brachinus*). This species has rust-red markings and the habit of discharging puffs of irritating, smoke-like gas from its anal opening which, no doubt, has a protective function.

Larval ground beetles are dark in color, have flattened bodies, and run rapidly. Like the adults, they are predacious on soft-bodied insects. They live in the same places as the adults.

Below: Ground beetles capture and feed upon cutworms and other insects. (Life size: 1 inch) Right top: This bombardier beetle employs an unusual means of defense. It puffs irritating, smoke-like gas from its tail. (Life size: 1 inch) Bottom: Like the adults, ground beetle larvae capture and eat insects. This one was found under a stone. (Life size: 1 inch)

Water beetles live in ponds and streams, using their long oar-like legs for swimming. Sometimes they leave the water and fly about. (Life size: 1 inch)

Larval water beetles are often called "water tigers" because they capture and eat other insects. (Life size: 1-1/2 inches)

FAMILY DYTISCIDAE—THE WATER BEETLES

There are several kinds of water beetles, but these are the most common. Some are more than an inch long and swim rapidly through the water by means of their oar-like legs. They capture and feed upon other water insects.

These beetles can remain submerged for long periods, but they often rise to the surface where they hang suspended, with their tails just breaking the surface film. Sometimes they leave the water and fly to bright lights.

Larval water beetles are elongate and have long sickle-like jaws used for capturing aquatic insects. Sometimes they are called "water tigers." The adults lay their eggs on underwater objects or insert them into the stems of water plants.

71

Firefly beetles have light-producing organs in their abdomens. Their flashing lights are aids in bringing the sexes together. (Life size 1/2 inch)

Larval firefly beetles feed upon snails and other soft-bodied creatures. Sometimes they are called "glow-worms." (Life size 1/2 inch)

FAMILY LAMPYRIDAE—THE FIREFLY BEETLES

These are perhaps the most remarkable of all beetles, since both as larvae and as adults they possess the ability to produce light.

Most species are winged and have *photogenic* or light-producing organs in their abdomens. Usually they are active at dusk, when they may be seen flashing their lights over marshes or grassy areas. The lights enable the males and females to locate each other.

Larval fireflies live upon the ground, especially in damp places, and are called "glowworms." They have flattened, segmented bodies, and feed upon snails and other soft-bodied creatures.

FAMILY ELATERIDAE—THE CLICK BEETLES

These beetles are more or less flattened and elongate in form. They vary in size from very tiny to giants nearly three inches in length. Most are about an inch long. Certain tropical species have light-generating organs. Another unusual characteristic of these beetles is the presence of a spine on the undersurface of one segment of the thorax that fits into a notched groove on another segment of the thorax. The beetle is able to bend its body up and down, causing the spine to snap in and out of the groove. When captured by a bird or grasped between the fingers, this snapping motion is usually sufficient to free it. If one of these beetles is placed on its back, it can snap its body, causing it to flip several inches into the air. If the first flip does not land it on its feet, it will continue to snap its body until it is successful.

Larval click beetles are slender and hard-bodied, and live in the soil or in rotting logs. They are usually called "wireworms." Some kinds are destructive to crops. When full grown they pupate in the places where they live.

This two-inch click beetle lived along the Amazon River of South America. Like all click beetles, it can snap its body at the center. (Life size: 2 inches)

Larval click beetles have hard, elongate bodies. They live in rotten logs or in the soil. They are called "wireworms." (Life size: 1 inch)

Metallic wood-boring beetles are usually brightly colored in metallic hues. This one, bright green in color, was collected along the Amazon River. (Life size: 2 inches)

Larval metallic wood borers have the front ends of their bodies enlarged. They bore under the bark of dead trees. (Life size: 1 inch)

FAMILY BUPRESTIDAE—THE METALLIC WOOD-BORING BEETLES

Beetles belonging to this family are shaped very much like those of the Elateridae family, but are frequently arrayed in bright metallic colors, being blue, green, or reddish.

They lay their eggs in the bark of trees and, upon hatching, the legless larvae tunnel under the bark. These larvae are easily recognized, since the front portions of their bodies are enlarged and flattened. They pupate in the tunnels where they have fed.

FAMILY COCCINELLIDAE—THE LADYBIRD BEETLES

These are the small, oval beetles, often with bright markings, frequently seen on plants. Many are red with black spots and are known as ladybugs, although they are not bugs. Most kinds feed upon aphids or plant lice, and so are beneficial to us. A few are plant-eaters. An example is the bean ladybeetle (*Epilachna corrupta*).

The larval beetles remind one of miniature alligators, and most kinds eat aphids. When mature they pupate on the plants where they have fed upon aphids or upon the plants whose leaves they have eaten.

Ladybird beetles are colorful little insects that feed upon aphids. Many kinds are spotted. (Life size: 1/4 inch)

Ladybird beetle larvae feed upon aphids like the adults. They are thus beneficial to us. (Life size: 1/8 inch)

75

Scarab beetles vary in size from minute to more than three inches. This one is the June beetle (*Polyphylla*). Note the special kind of antennae. (Life size: 1 inch)

Scarab beetle larvae are usually of C-form and are called grubs. Most kinds live in the ground and feed upon plant roots. (Life size: 1 inch)

FAMILY SCARABAEIDAE—THE SCARAB BEETLES

There are many kinds of scarab beetles and their food habits vary. Some are of small size but others are among our largest insects. The largest scarab found in the United States is the giant rhinoceros beetle (*Dynastes*) which is more than two inches long and very heavy-bodied. It bears a horn on the upper, forward portion of its body, the reason for its name, rhinoceros. Even larger scarabs occur in tropical lands. Their large larvae (grubs) live in rotting wood.

Other scarabs, such as the common June beetles and May beetles, are of moderate size. The life histories of these latter beetles are typical of many kinds. They lay their eggs in the ground where their white, grub-like larvae feed upon plant roots, often causing damage to the plants. These larvae have legs and their bodies are curved in the form of a C.

Other scarabs feed upon animal dung and are known as dung beetles. Sometimes these busy little beetles are seen rolling balls of dung about on the ground. Eventually these balls are buried and eggs laid in them. It is here that the larvae feed and develop.

Members of the Scarabaeidae family are stout-bodied and have a special kind of antennae composed of thin plates. Such antennae are said to be *lamellate* in form.

This is the pupa of the green June beetle *(Cotinus)* seen in its cell in the ground. (Life size: 1 inch)

A green June beetle just changed into the adult stage. It will soon leave its cell and come up above the ground.

Left: Long-horned beetles are usually found in forested areas where their larvae bore in trees. This one was found along the Amazon River. (Life size: 2 inches)

Right: The adult female twig girdler (*Oncideres*) cuts a neat groove around a twig. She then lays an egg in the end of the twig and when the twig dies and falls to the ground, her larva lives and bores in it. (Life size: 1 inch)

Bottom: Larval long-horned beetles bore into dead trees and their limbs. (Life size: 1 inch)

FAMILY CERAMBYCIDAE—THE LONG-HORNED BEETLES

These insects have very long antennae, the reason they are called "long-horned" beetles. There are many kinds and they frequent woods and forests where their larvae bore into trees. The adults are often seen on flowers, feeding on pollen or nectar. Some kinds have powerful jaws and may bite if handled. Many long-horned beetles are of large size and may be brightly colored.

These beetles lay their eggs in trees and the larvae bore into the wood, creating round tunnels. The larvae are elongate and white in color. Pupation takes place in the tunnels. At least a year is required for completion of their life histories. Some take much longer.

Of special interest are the twig girdlers (*Oncideres*). When ready to lay her eggs, the female selects a twig and cuts a deep groove around it. She then lays an egg in the tip of the twig. Eventually the twig dies and breaks off at the site of the groove. Upon the ground, the larval beetle bores into the now-dead twig and completes its growth, and pupates.

FAMILY CURCULIONIDAE—THE WEEVILS

These are the snout-beetles, easily recognized, since they have the front portion of their heads prolonged into snouts. The antennae are located on the snout. They vary in size from tiny to nearly two inches in length in some tropical species. The average size for North American species is probably about a quarter of an inch long. The length of the snout is variable. In some, such as the acorn weevil, it may be as long as the body.

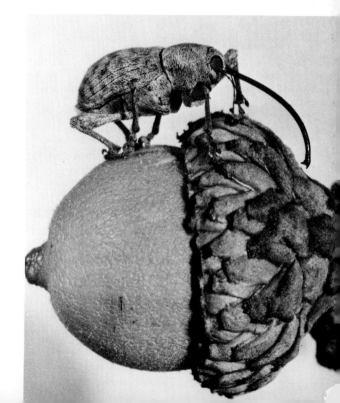

This adult female acorn weevil has a long snout used to feed in oak acorns. Her larvae are plump grubs that live and feed inside acorns. (Life size: 1/2 inch)

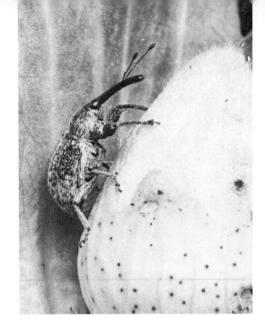

Left: The boll weevil is the most serious pest of cotton. This adult boll weevil is perched on a cotton bud. Its larvae feed inside. (Life size: 1/4 inch)

Right: This cotton "square" or flower bud has been cut open to expose a pupal boll weevil inside. (Life size, pupa: 1/4 inch)

Both adults and larvae are plant-eaters, feeding upon almost every part of their preferred host plants. Since there are numerous species, feeding upon a wide variety of plants, their life histories vary greatly. They may pass the winter in any stage.

Fairly typical of their life histories is that of the well-known cotton boll weevil (*Anthonomus grandis*). The adult females, having over-wintered in trash in hedgerows, feed upon the young cotton "squares" or flower buds, using their snouts for the purpose. They lay their eggs in these feeding punctures, and the larvae develop in the maturing "squares." Here pupation occurs and the first generation of adults emerges. These adults feed upon the cotton bolls or seed pods, and lay their eggs in the feeding punctures. The next generation of larvae matures inside the bolls, causing great damage to them.

ORDER LEPIDOPTERA—BUTTERFLIES AND MOTHS

The members of this order are easily recognized and familiar to everyone. They are winged and their wings are covered with scales. It is the coloration of these microscopic scales that impart the attractive patterns to their wings, and these scales are the reason for the order name, Lepidoptera, a term of Greek origin meaning "scale-winged."

The larval insects, usually called caterpillars, have legs and chewing mouthparts. The adults have slender sucking mouthparts that are usually coiled under their heads when not in use. The adults usually feed upon flower nectar, while the larvae are plant-eaters.

This order is divided into two groups: the moths and the butterflies.

THE BUTTERFLIES—These insects are characterized by having clubs at the tips of their antennae. When at rest their wings are closed over their backs but not folded. Most of them are *diurnal;* that is, they are active by day. Their larvae or caterpillars rarely spin cocoons. Thus, their pupae are usually naked and are called *chrysalids.*

Left: Butterfly eggs are of many forms, colors, and sizes. This is the egg of the cabbage butterfly. (Life size: 1/64 inch)

Right: Tent caterpillar moths *(Malacosoma)* lay their eggs in masses surrounding twigs. Winter is passed in this stage. (Life size: 1/2 inch)

Some caterpillars are very small. This one, the larva of a tiny moth, tunnels between the upper and lower surfaces of a leaf. It is called a "leaf miner." (Life size 1/8 inch)

The large caterpillar of the regal moth (*Citheronia*) feeds on hickory and is known as the hickory horned-devil. It looks dangerous but is harmless. (Life size: 5 inches)

FAMILY PAPILIONIDAE—

THE SWALLOWTAIL BUTTERFLIES

The swallowtails are the largest and most attractive of our butterflies. They are found almost everywhere. Probably the most common species is the handsome tiger swallowtail (*Papilio glaucus*). Its caterpillars feed upon birch, poplar, and other trees. When full-grown, they are dark green and have an eye-spot on each side of the third segment back of the head. These spots are yellow edged with black.

82

The tiger swallowtail is prabably our best known and most attractive butterfly. Its caterpillars feed upon the foliage of various trees. (Life size: 4 inches)

The caterpillars of swallowtail butterflies are devoid of spines, but some kinds have *osmeteria* or scent glands. Their chrysalids are suspended from, or attached to, various objects, and it is in this stage that winter is passed.

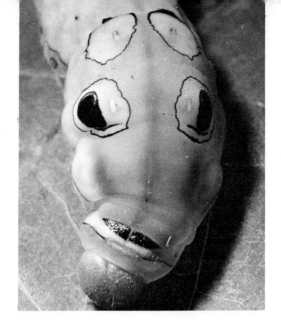

Below right: Swallowtail butterfly chrysalids are suspended from twigs or other objects by means of a sling. (Life size: 1 inch)

Below: The caterpillar of the black swallowtail butterfly (*Papilio ajax*) is green with black bands set with orange spots. When alarmed it pushes out two orange scent glands. It feeds on plants of the carrot family. (Life size: 1-1/2 inches)

Above: This view of the forward portion of the caterpillar of the spicebush swallowtail (*Papilio troilus*) shows its eye-spots. It is believed that these may frighten enemies away. These caterpillars feed on sassafras and other plants. (Life size: 1-1/2 inches)

FAMILY PIERIDAE—THE WHITE AND SULFUR BUTTERFLIES

These moderate-sized butterflies are either white with black, orange, or red markings, or yellow with dark markings. They range in size from one to three inches across. Probably the most widespread species is the imported cabbage butterfly (*Pieris rapae*), a white butterfly with black markings. Its greenish caterpillars feed upon cabbage and related plants. Another one is the orange sulfur (*Colias eurytheme*), whose greenish caterpillars feed on clover and other plants of the legume family. In the Southeast there occurs the large cloudless sulfur (*C. sennae*) that is often seen migrating in a southeasterly direction in autumn. Its caterpillars are greenish with dark markings, and feed upon wild senna.

Left: The dog's-head butterfly (*Zerene caesonia*) is a sulfur butterfly of yellow and black. Its caterpillars feed on clover. (Life size: 1-1/2 inches) Center: Here an egg of the cabbage butterfly has just hatched into a tiny cater-pillar. (Life size: 1/64 inch) Right: This is the adult cabbage butterfly *(Pieris rapae)*. It is black and white. Its caterpillars are green "worms" that feed on cabbage. (Life size: 1-1/4 inches)

Left: Monarch butterfly in flight. These butterflies often migrate long distances. (Life size: 2-1/2 inches) Right: Monarch butterfly caterpillars feed upon milkweed and are banded with yellow and black. (Life size: 1-1/4 inches) Bottom: Here a monarch caterpillar has suspended itself from a patch of silk. Soon it will shed its skin and change into a chrysalid. (Life size: 1-1/4 inches)

FAMILY DANAIDAE—THE MILKWEED BUTTERFLIES

To this family belongs the well-known monarch butterfly (*Danaus plexippus*). These butterflies measure nearly four inches across and are rust-red, marked with black. They are of special interest because of their migratory habits. As an example, one specimen, tagged in Canada, was later recaptured in Central Mexico. Normally these butterflies migrate southward in autumn, often in large numbers, and congregate in southern areas. In spring they fly northward, laying their eggs on milkweed. Eventually they reach Canada. The eggs laid on milkweed hatch into caterpillars having two slender appendages at each end, and their bodies banded with yellow, black, and white. The chrysalids are vivid green with gold markings and are suspended from milkweed leaves or other nearby objects. Upon emerging, the adults fly northward. Late in summer they start southward.

FAMILY HESPERIIDAE—THE SKIPPER BUTTERFLIES

Skipper butterflies are of small or medium size and, when at rest, partly fold their wings. As in all butterflies, their antennae have terminal clubs, but beyond the club there is, in this case, a sharp, curved tip. Their bodies are large in proportion to their wings and they fly rapidly.

Some skippers are brightly colored but the most common kinds are rust-red, marked with black.

Larval skippers are smooth-bodied and have large heads and narrow necks. Many kinds construct leaf shelters by rolling up leaves and fastening them together with silk. They pupate in silken cocoons.

Below: Skipper butterflies fold their wings over their backs when at rest. They fly very rapidly. (Life size: 1 inch across) Right: Skipper butterfly caterpillars have narrow necks and feed on various plants. During the day they enclose themselves in rolled-up leaves. (Life size: 1 inch) Bottom: This head-on view of a skipper butterfly makes it look like an antlered deer. Note the large eyes and the sharp tips on the antennae.

THE MOTHS—Moths usually fold their wings when at rest and their antennae are thread-like or feather-like. Only rarely are the antennae clubbed at the tip. Most moths are *nocturnal,* or night-active, and often attracted to lights. There are thousands of different kinds and they range in size from minute to six inches across.

Their larvae are caterpillars similar to those of butterflies, but their pupae are usually enclosed in silken cocoons.

FAMILY SATURNIIDAE—THE GIANT SILK MOTHS

The members of this family are the largest of all moths. Most kinds have a wing expanse of three or more inches. A few are smaller. Many kinds are vividly colored and rival the butterflies in beauty. The antennae of the males are feather-like. The largest saturniid in the United States is the common cecropia moth (*Samia cecropia*). It is reddish brown with various markings, including eye-spots at the tips of the front wings. They range in size from five to six inches across. The caterpillars, when full grown, are nearly four inches long, green in color, and armed with six rows of *tubercules* or blunt spines. They feed upon a wide variety of trees and the silken cocoons are attached lengthwise to the twigs.

The large green luna moth is probably our most beautiful moth. (Life size: wingspread, 4-1/2 inches)

87

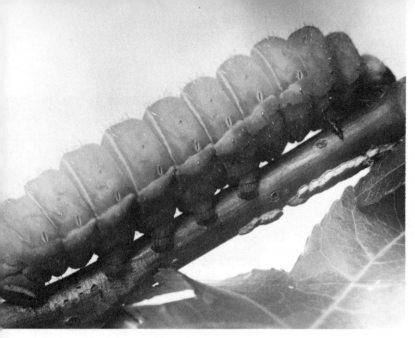

Luna moth caterpillars are green in color and feed on the leaves of various trees. (Life size: 1-1/2 inches)

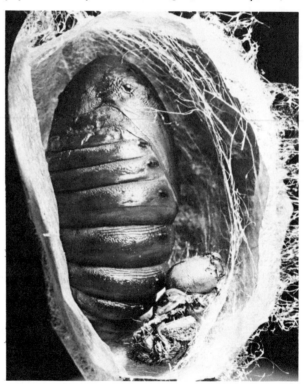

Here a luna cocoon has been cut open to expose the pupa. Winter is passed in this stage. (Life size: 2 inches)

Probably the most beautiful of these large moths is the luna moth (*Tropaea luna*), a large green species with long tails on its hind wings. Its caterpillar is about three inches long, and blue-green with a pale yellow stripe along each side of its body. The caterpillars feed upon the foliage of various trees.

88

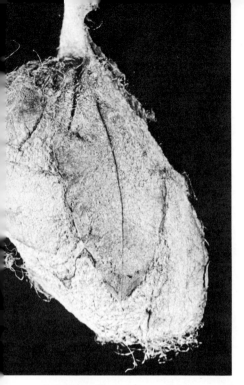

Left: The silken cocoon of the promethea moth *(Callosamia promethea)* is enclosed in a leaf. (Life size: 2 inches)

Center: This photo shows a promethea moth just emerged from its cocoon. Its wings have not fully expanded. (Life size: wingspread, 4 inches across)

Right: An hour later the promethea's wings have expanded and it will soon be ready to fly.

FAMILY SPHINGIDAE—THE SPHINX MOTHS

These are the moths often seen hovering in front of deep-throated flowers at dusk. They remind one of hummingbirds and are often called hummingbird moths. Their bodies are large and spindle-shaped, and their wings are narrow. Some kinds are very attractive. In size they vary from two to five inches across.

The most common species is the tomato hornworm moth (*Protoparce quinquemaculata*). Its caterpillars have horn-like tails on the rear ends of their bodies, and feed upon tomato, tobacco, and

Left: Sphinx moths are often seen hovering at deep-throated flowers. They have heavy bodies and narrow wings. This one is the tersa sphinx *(Xylophanes tersa)*. (Life size: 2-1/4 inches) Below left: Sphinx moth caterpillars are of various forms. This is the caterpillar of the pandora sphinx *(Pholus)*. When young it has a horn-like tail. It feeds on grape. (Life size: 1-1/2 inches) Right: This is the tobacco hornworm caterpillar *(Protoparce)*. It is a pest of tobacco. Note the horn on its tail. Also note the cocoons of parasitic wasps on its body. (Life size: 2 inches)

potato, often causing damage. The presence of the tails is the reason for their common name, "hornworm."

There are a number of other sphinx moths, most of which have similar habits, except for differences in food. The caterpillars of some have eye-spots instead of tails on the rear ends of their bodies. In most cases, when ready to pupate, the caterpillars burrow into the ground and change into pupae having pitcher-like "handles." These underground pupae are not enclosed in cocoons. Winter is usually passed in this stage. The moths emerge in spring and lay their eggs on preferred food plants.

FAMILY ARCTIIDAE—THE TIGER MOTHS

These medium-sized moths are bright, striped or spotted in contrasting colors. When at rest they fold their wings roof-like over their backs. In some cases the hind wings are colored differently from the front wings. One of the best known members of the family is the woolly bear (*Isia isabella*), also known as the Isabella tiger moth. It is the woolly caterpillar of this moth that gives it the name "woolly bear." These caterpillars are black at each end and rust-red in the middle, a feature that gave rise to an old superstition. In autumn these caterpillars are often seen crawling rapidly across highways and mountain trails. It is believed by some that the width of the reddish, middle band indicates the length of the coming winter. The truth is that these caterpillars have no advance warning concerning the duration of the winter; they are, however, hurrying to find a suitable place to hibernate until spring. This may be under a fallen log or beneath the bark of a dead tree. With the arrival of spring they will spin cocoons consisting of silk mixed with hairs from their bodies. The adult

Left: Most tiger moths are strikingly marked and have colorful hind wings. (Life size: 1-1/4 inches)

Above: Tiger moth caterpillars are very hairy and usually called "woolly bears." Winter is passed in the caterpillar stage. (Life size: 1 inch)

females lay their eggs on various weeds and the young caterpillars feed upon them.

Another tiger moth is the fall webworm moth (*Hypantria cunea*). These moths are snow-white and lay their eggs in clusters on the foliage of various trees and shrubs. When the hairy larvae hatch, they remain together, spinning a large silken web in which they all live, protected from most enemies.

FAMILY GEOMETRIDAE—THE MEASURINGWORM MOTHS

This is a large family of slender-bodied moths, usually having angular wings. These wings are tan, brown, or sometimes green, marked with lines or bands.

It is the larvae of these moths that are of special interest. Often called "inchworms" or "measuringworms," they crawl about in a looping fashion. Some kinds are serious pests of forests and gardens. Some of the caterpillars have the habit of posing on twigs as if they were merely another twig. This probably helps them to elude the eyes of birds.

The cocoons of these insects are flimsy affairs attached to leaves. Some kinds bore into the ground to pupate and do not spin cocoons.

Below: Measuringworm moths usually have angular wings. The markings of this one make it blend with the bark upon which it rests. (Life size: 1 inch) Right: Measuringworm caterpillars crawl by looping motions. They often rest on plants, appearing as if they were twigs. (Life size: 1 inch)

Above: This is the puss moth caterpillar, the larval stage of a flannel moth (Megalopyge opercularis). Beneath its silky brown hair are many poison spines. (Life size: 1 inch)

Right: The cocoon of the puss moth is fitted with a lid through which the adult can escape. The adult is a brownish moth. (Life size: 1 inch)

FAMILY MEGALOPYGIDAE—THE FLANNEL MOTHS

The adults are robust in form and brownish-yellow in color. They are about an inch across. Their caterpillars are found on a variety of trees and shrubs, and are covered with soft brown hair. Beneath this hair are many poison spines which have a protective function. Because of their hairy covering these caterpillars are usually called "puss caterpillars."

When mature the caterpillars spin characteristic cocoons attached to twigs. The cocoon has a lid at one end through which the adult escapes after emerging from its pupal case. The most common kind is *Megalopyge opercularis*.

FAMILY EUCLEIDAE—THE SLUG CATERPILLAR MOTHS

The larvae of these moths are called "slug caterpillars" because they are short and slug-like and creep slowly about on leaves. Some are brightly colored and many kinds are covered with sharp, poisonous spines which are protective. The moths are robust and very hairy. Some are quite colorful.

One of the easiest to recognize is the saddleback caterpillar (*Sibine stimulea*) that feeds on various trees and shrubs. These caterpillars are about an inch long and green in color. In the center of their backs is a brownish "saddle" centered with orange. Each end of the body bears many needlelike spines containing a powerful poison. They are dangerous to handle. The striking colors of these larvae is known as *warning coloration* and warns any enemy that they had best be let alone. They are common in the Southeast, usually in autumn. The moths are brown with green markings on the wings.

Other slug caterpillars are frequently found on oaks. They have flattened bodies, are often greenish, and are covered with poisonous spines. They have the habit of clinging to the undersides of leaves, and people are often stung when handling the leaves.

Saddleback caterpillars are green with an orange spot bordered with white on their backs. Their spines contain powerful poison. (Life size: 3/4 inch)

Many slug caterpillars are greenish and covered with poison spines. They are found on plants of many kinds. (Life size: 1/2 inch)

This is the adult moth of the army worm caterpillar *(Cirphis unipuncta)*. Its caterpillars, a type of cutworm, are important crop pests. (Life size: 1-1/2 inches)

Many kinds of cutworm caterpillars are pests of gardens and field crops. This is a typical cutworm. It will pupate in the ground and spend the winter there. (Life size: 1 inch)

FAMILY NOCTUIDAE (PHALAENIDAE)—THE MILLERS

The family Noctuidae is sometimes called family Phalaenidae, but whichever name is used, these are the common millers often attracted to lights. Moths of other kinds are also attracted to lights, but these are the ones seen most often. Most kinds are about an inch across and of dull coloration. The largest is a tropical species that sometimes flies northward into the United States. This is the black witch *(Erebus odora)* which measures up to five inches across.

The caterpillars of these moths are usually called "cutworms" and some are very injurious to crops and gardens. One is the army worm *(Cirphis unipuncta)*. Another is the caterpillar often found feeding in ears of corn. This is the corn earworm *(Heliothis armigera)*. In most cases these caterpillars burrow into the ground and pupate there. Winter is usually passed in this stage.

ORDER DIPTERA—TWO-WINGED FLIES

Included here are the true two-winged flies. Insects of other kinds are frequently called "flies," but this term should properly be applied only to members of the order Diptera. All these insects have but two wings. These are the front wings, the hind wings being reduced to small knob-like organs called *halteres* which apparently function as balancing or gyroscopic sense organs. When these organs are removed the insects cannot fly properly. Even though these insects possess only two wings, they are among the world's fastest fliers, some having been clocked at over fifty miles per hour. Not only can they fly very rapidly, but they can maneuver with great skill, darting swiftly and then hovering in the air as if suspended on invisible strings.

Some flies have piercing-sucking mouthparts. Others do not feed at all during their adult stages.

The habits of flies and their larvae vary greatly. Mosquitoes pierce the skins of animals and siphon out their blood. Larval mosquitoes dwell in the water where they feed upon organic matter or on living aquatic life. Bot fly larvae are parasitic in the bodies of horses, cattle, and other animals. Many live as parasites in other insects. Many flies and their larvae are scavengers. The housefly is an example.

The hind wings of flies are reduced to tiny balancing organs (arrow). In flight these organs *(halteres)* vibrate rapidly and serve as gyroscopic sense organs. (Life size, fly: 1 inch)

This parasitic fly has just emerged from its pupal case or *puparium*. As a larva it was parasitic in a cutworm. (Life size: 1/4 inch)

A close-up of a horsefly's eye shows the upper portion made up of large facets, adapted for distant vision. The lower part has smaller facets for near vision.

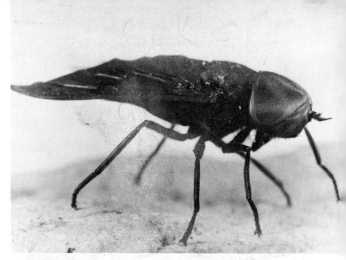

Horseflies have mouthparts fitted for sucking blood. They are pests of livestock and humans. Their larvae live in the soil. (Life size: 1 inch)

FAMILY TABANIDAE—THE HORSEFLIES

Horseflies vary in size from perhaps a quarter to half an inch long. Some kinds feed chiefly upon pollen and nectar from flowers, but others have blood-sucking habits which give these insects their importance. Not only do they annoy man and animals by sucking their blood, but some kinds transmit diseases such as tularemia and anthrax.

Tabanid females lay their eggs in or near water and the spindle-shaped larvae live in the water or in the damp soil surrounding pools. They feed upon other insects or worms. To this family also belong the deer flies.

FAMILY CULICIDAE—THE MOSQUITOES

This is a large group of flies having the blood-sucking habit. Since they fly from animal to animal, many kinds transmit diseases. These include some of the world's most important human diseases such as yellow fever, malaria, and dengue fever. Most adult mosquitoes are active at night.

Larval mosquitoes, called "wrigglers," live in the water of ponds, pools, or artifical containers such as old water-filled cans. Certain tropical species live in water contained in the leaf-axils of air-plants high in trees. They feed upon algae or on dead organic matter. A few kinds are predacious on other mosquito larvae. The larvae are air-breathers, rising to the surface now and then to obtain their oxygen.

Pupal mosquitoes are called "tumblers." They are very active but do not feed. When the adults emerge, they mate and the females lay their eggs together in "rafts," or singly, on aquatic plants growing in or near the water.

Right: Larval mosquitoes or "wrigglers" live in the water. Those shown are resting at the water's surface with their breathing tubes or *siphons* touching the surface film. (Life size: 1/4 inch)
Above: Pupal mosquitoes or "tumblers" are active but do not feed.

FAMILY ASILIDAE—THE ROBBER FLIES

These moderate-sized flies are highly predacious, capturing and feeding upon insects that are often larger than themselves. Some robber flies are very hairy and resemble bumblebees.

Larval robber flies live in the ground where they feed upon the larvae of other insects.

Top: In this unusual photo an adult mosquito is emerging from the pupa or "tumbler." It was photographed through the wall of a small aquarium. (Life size: 1/4 inch)

Left: Close-up of an adult mosquito. (Life size: 1/4 inch)

Below: Robber flies prey on other insects. Their larvae live in the ground or in decaying wood. (Life size: 1 inch)

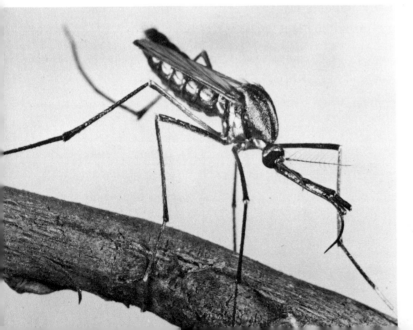

Syrphid flies are often seen on flowers. Their larvae feed upon aphids living on plants. Some kinds live in the soil. (Life size: 1/2 inch)

Here such a maggot-like larva of a syrphid fly has captured an adult aphid and is feeding on it. Note the other aphids in the background.

FAMILY SYRPHIDAE—THE FLOWER FLIES

These flies are often seen hovering over flowers, and feeding on their nectar. Many kinds are brightly colored and remind one of bees or wasps.

The larvae of many kinds are predacious on aphids. It is not unusual to see these maggot-like larvae among groups of aphids living on leaves and stems. Others are scavengers in polluted habitats. The larvae of one kind, the drone fly (*Eristalis*), is the rat-tailed maggot sometimes found in water. It has a long breathing tube attached to its rear end.

101

FAMILY TRYPETIDAE—THE FRUIT FLIES

These small flies have "pictured" wings, that is, their wings are spotted or banded in attractive patterns. They are frequently seen perched on flowers or leaves, slowly moving their wings up and down.

In most cases the larvae bore into plants or fruit, often causing damage. The larvae of one kind (*Rhagoletis*) is an apple maggot. Another pest species is the Mediterranean fruit fly (*Ceratitis capitata*) which infests citrus fruit. An interesting species is the goldenrod gall fly (*Eurosta*) whose larvae form the enlarged galls often seen on the stems of goldenrod plants.

The goldenrod gall fly has "pictured" wings. (Life size: 1/2 inch) The photographs on the following page show the life history of the goldenrod gall fly.

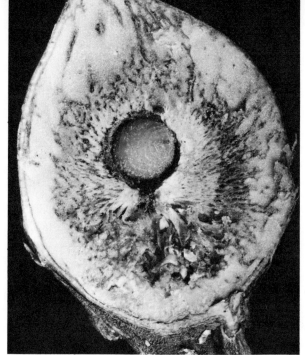

Above: These enlargements, or galls, were produced on goldenrod stems by the larvae of gall flies living inside. (Life size: 1 inch)

Top right: Here a goldenrod gall has been cut open to show the larval fly inside.

Bottom: This is a goldenrod gall fly pupa in the gall. (Life size, pupa: 1/4 inch)

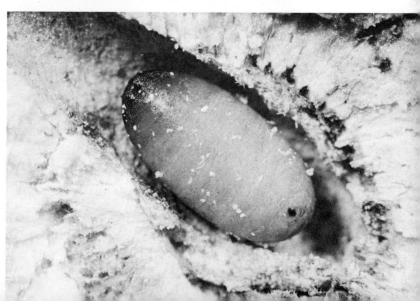

FAMILY MUSCIDAE—THE HOUSEFLIES

These small to medium-sized flies occur in almost all parts of the world. There are many different kinds, some of which are pests. Best known is the common housefly (*Musca domestica*) whose maggot-like larvae develop in decaying materials of almost all kinds. Since these flies develop in filth, they are believed to carry typhoid fever, dysentery, cholera, and other human diseases.

Houseflies do not bite, but some other members of the family do. Examples are the stable fly (*Stomoxys calcitrans*) and the horn fly (*Siphona irritans*). The famous tsetse fly (*Glossina*) of Africa, the carrier of sleeping sickness, also belongs to this family.

Left: Houseflies are among the most common of all insects. They are pests in many lands. (Life size: 1/4 inch)
Below: Larval houseflies (maggots) usually live and feed in decaying materials. They are white and legless. The head end is at the left. (Life size: 1/4 inch)

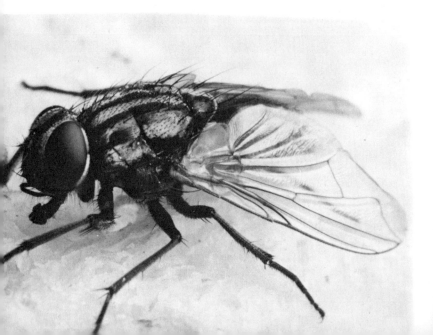

ORDER HYMENOPTERA—ANTS, BEES, WASPS, AND HORNETS

To this large and important order belong many common insects. Some are injurious to us, while others, such as honeybees, are very useful. Many hymenopterous insects are beneficial to man because they are parasitic on harmful pests. Bees pollinate flowers and are thus of value to us.

Most of these insects are winged and their four wings are thin and membranous. A few, including worker ants, are wingless. They have chewing-biting mouthparts, although the mouthparts of most bees are also fitted for sucking out the nectar of flowers. Many kinds have stings and poison glands.

The larvae of these insects are varied in habits; some have legs and resemble caterpillars, other are legless and grub-like. The pupae are, in some cases, enclosed in silken cocoons.

Among these are some of the most "intelligent" of all insects. In some there are well-developed systems of communication and many are skillful craftsmen.

Bees of most kinds are important from the standpoint of flower pollination. Without bees many plants would not produce seeds. This bumblebee pollinates a passion flower bloom. (Life size, bee: 1 inch)

An *Ammophila* wasp uses a pebble to hammer down the sand over her underground nest tunnel. This is one of the few instances of an insect using a "tool." (Life size: 1 inch)

105

The social way of life reaches its peak among the ants, bees, and hornets, many of which live together in populous colonies in which the caste system is highly developed.

There are many families, but the following are the most important.

FAMILY BRACONIDAE—THE PARASITIC WASPS

These tiny wasps are mostly parasitic. Some kinds parasitize caterpillars, others are parasites of aphids. Many are so small that their larvae are able to mature inside the eggs of certain insects.

Most unusual are the habits of certain braconids (*Macrocentrus*). In this case the tiny female wasp deposits an egg in a caterpillar. When this egg hatches, it develops into many larvae instead of just one. After feeding on the inner tissues of the caterpillar they become

A braconid wasp laid an egg in this hornworm caterpillar. From this one egg numerous wasp larvae developed and, when they were full grown, emerged from the caterpillar and spun cocoons. (Life size, caterpillar: 2 inches)

Left: In this photograph most of the wasps have emerged from their cocoons on the caterpillar.

Above: This braconid wasp adult was photographed in the act of emerging from its silken cocoon. (Life size: 1/16 inch)

mature and emerge through the host's skin. They then spin their tiny silken cocoons. It is not unusual to see such a parasitized caterpillar with numerous white wasp cocoons attached to it. The caterpillar will die before pupating. I have counted nearly a thousand such wasp cocoons on a single caterpillar. The production of many larvae from one egg is called *polyembryony*.

FAMILY CYNIPIDAE—THE GALL WASPS

There are numerous kinds of gall wasps and many of them have most unusual life histories. They are very small in size, and are remarkable because their larvae produce galls or abnormal growths on plants.

In these wasps there is an *alternation of generations*. In other words, the individuals of one generation of wasps do not resemble their parents, but are like their grandparents. Their life histories are thus quite complex. An example is the spiny hedgehog gall (*Acraspis erinacei*) often seen on oak leaves. These spherical galls attached to the leaves contain from two to eight larval wasps. The gall itself was caused to grow on the leaf by a substance secreted

Galls are caused to grow on many plants by tiny gall wasps. This is a hedgehog gall, created on an oak leaf by a cynipid wasp larva. (Life size: 1/2 inch)

Plant galls of many kinds and colors are created on various plants by gall-making insects. Galls may be found on almost all parts of trees and plants.

108

by the larvae. Eventually all of these larvae transform into adult wasps, all females. Without mating, these females deposit their eggs in the buds of the oak. The following spring, small galls are produced on the buds, each one containing a larval wasp. The adult wasps that emerge from these bud galls are very different from their mothers and are both males and females. After maturing, the females of this generation lay their eggs in young oak leaves and the typical hedgehog galls are produced by the larvae living inside. When these larvae transform into adult wasps, eggs are laid in oak leaves and the cycle starts over again.

Not all gall wasps have this type of life history, but many do.

Here an adult cynipid wasp has just emerged from its cell. (Life size, wasp: 1/16 inch)

Larval gall wasps are grub-like. This is a gall wasp pupa removed from its cell in a gall. (Life size: 1/16 inch)

A queen flies above a marching column of African driver ants *(Dorylus)* made up of small workers and large-jawed soldiers. (Life size, queen: 1-1/4 inch)

Wingless worker ants do the work of the colony. Here two worker carpenter ants *(Camponotus)* care for larval ants in a tunnel cut in a twig. (Life size, workers: 1/4 inch)

FAMILY FORMICIDAE—THE ANTS

Ants of various kinds have been known and studied for thousands of years. They are mentioned in the Bible many times. Probably no other group of insects is so widely distributed. There are nearly a thousand different species in the world, but they are especially abundant in warm climates.

Ants all have social habits, that is, they live in colonies often containing thousands of individuals. Usually these colonies are made up of at least three castes; queens, males, and imperfect females or workers. In most cases there is but a single queen, the individual that lays all the eggs. She is the only mated queen. Males usually are present only at certain

110

seasons. All the other ants in a colony are workers. Only the queens and males have wings.

The harvester ants *(Pogonomyrmex)* may be taken as a typical example. These ants nest in the ground, building mounds rising nearly a foot above the level of the surrounding area. The workers gather seeds from nearby plants and carry them into the underground passages where they are stored and serve as food for the entire colony.

At certain seasons, large numbers of winged queens and males are produced. These swarm out of the nest and mate. Usually the queens mate with males of other colonies. Having mated, the males die, but the mated queens excavate small tunnels in the ground, cut off their wings, and begin laying eggs. In this manner each queen starts a new colony. The first larvae are fed and cared for by the queen, but later, she has the help of the workers that develop from the first eggs. The colony gradually increases in size. It is always the workers who do all the work from then on. They gather food, excavate new tunnels, and feed and care for the grub-like young.

Ant colonies of other kinds are found in a wide variety of situations and feed upon various foods. Many nest in trees, under stones, in rotten logs, or in human habitations. Some ants, such as tropical leaf-cutting ants *(Atta)*, actually cultivate fungi in underground cavities and they and their larvae feed upon the fungus. There are many pest species.

Left: This is a close-up of a larval harvester ant. Right: Pupal ants are white and helpless. Soon this pupal har- vester ant *(Pogonomyrmex)* will shed its outer skin and change into a worker. (Life size: 1/4 inch)

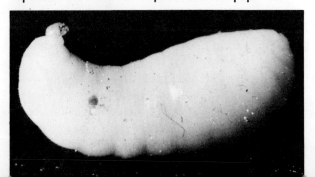

FAMILY VESPIDAE—THE HORNETS AND YELLOWJACKETS

These insects are of medium-to-large size and live in colonies consisting of males (drones), queens, and workers. Usually but one queen is present, and drones are present only during certain seasons. All the workers have stings. In general, there are two types of vespids: ground-living yellowjackets and paper-nest hornets that build their nests in trees.

The tree-nesting hornet *(Vespula maculata)* is a typical example of the family. Almost everyone is familiar with their large paper nests suspended from the branches of trees. These nests have walls made up of several layers of gray paper. Inside such a nest are horizontal tiers of paper cells containing the larval hornets, which are white and legless. These larvae

Hornets of some kinds build paper nests in trees. This nest has been cut away to show the tiers of paper combs. (Life size: 1 foot)

Yellowjackets build their paper nests underground. Shown here are tiers of their paper combs, with a queen in the foreground. The cells contain developing larvae.

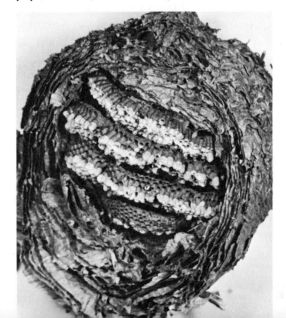

A close-up of the paper cells shows larval hornets in some cells and eggs in others. Also seen are a few capped cells containing pupae. (Life size, comb cells: 1/4 inch)

are fed and cared for by the workers. Some workers leave the nest during the day in search of caterpillars and other insects. These are chewed up into hamburger-like paste and carried back to the nest and fed to the hornet larvae in their cells.

When full-grown, the larvae are sealed in their cells and pupation occurs. In time, these transform into adult workers who cut their way out of the cells.

In late summer, males and females (queens) are produced, the queens resulting from fertilized eggs. These individuals soon leave the nest and mate. In time, the young queens find suitable locations, perhaps under a rotten log, and hibernate for the winter. With the arrival of spring each queen will establish a new colony. In the meantime, all the inhabitants of the old colony die, killed by the cold. Only the mated queens survive the winter.

The life histories of the yellowjackets—a type of hornet—are quite similar.

Left: Most sphex wasps stock their nests with spiders or insects as food for their young. This one has captured a grasshopper and is dragging it to her underground burrow. (Life size: 1 inch) Right: A mud dauber wasp collects a ball of clay for nest building. (Life size: 1 inch)

FAMILY SPHECIDAE—THE MUD DAUBERS AND DIGGER WASPS

This is a large family of nonsocial wasps having various nesting habits. The females construct nests and rear their young, but no colonies are formed and there is no worker caste. These are slender wasps, usually black or, sometimes, metallic blue or green. Some have yellow, orange, or red markings. They are thread-waisted.

Perhaps the most common of these wasps are the mud daubers *(Scliphron)* that construct clay or mud cells on porch ceilings, under ledges, or in other places protected from the weather. The female is slender, and black and yellow in color. She collects small balls of clay from a damp place and carries these to the chosen nest location. There she forms the clay into a neat cell having an opening at one end. About thirty loads of clay are needed to complete the cell.

After the cell is finished she goes spider hunting. When a spider is located she stings it, causing the spider to become paralyzed. It is then carried back and placed in the clay cell. She then goes hunting again and when she has stocked the cell with about half a dozen spiders, she lays an egg in the cell and then collects more clay to seal the opening. She then begins building another clay cell.

In the meantime her egg hatches and the white, legless larval wasp begins feeding upon the paralyzed spiders. When the larva has eaten all the spiders and become full grown, it pupates in the cell. Eventually it transforms into an adult wasp and cuts its way out of the protective clay cell. The males take no part in the nesting activities; their only function is the fertilization of the females.

Many other sphex wasps (members of the family Sphecidae) nest in tunnels they excavate in the ground. These ground-nesting species stock their nests with various insects that they paralyze with their stings. These include grasshoppers, crickets, flies, or other insects. In each case the larval wasps feed upon the insects so carefully placed in the nest tunnel by the mother wasp.

The clay cell of a mud dauber wasp broken open to show the paralyzed spiders and the larval wasp inside. (Life size of cell: 3/4 inch)

Another mason wasp is the potter wasp *(Eumenes)*. She stocks her clay cell with small caterpillars. (Life size, cell: 1/2 inch)

SUPERFAMILY APOIDEA—THE BEES

This special division, called a superfamily, contains a number of families of insects, all bee-like. They are small-to-large insects having hairy bodies. Usually they are orange, yellow, or black. Unlike most wasps, bees feed upon pollen and nectar collected from flowers. Some kinds lead solitary lives, other live in colonies.

FAMILY XYLOCOPIDAE—THE CARPENTER BEES

These bees are of moderate-to-large size and dark in color. The female cuts a deep tunnel in hard wood and stocks it with pollen and nectar. The male takes no part in the labor, but he does stay nearby, perhaps helping to guard the nest. When the larvae have consumed all the food, they change into pupae, then into adults. When ready to leave the nest tunnel, the mother leads them out and soon they are on their own.

Left: The female carpenter bee cuts tunnels in hard wood and stocks the individual cells with a mixture of pollen and nectar as food for her larvae. These bees resemble bumblebees. (Life size: 3/4 inch) Right: This cut-away view of a carpenter bee tunnel in wood shows the larval bees in their cells, separated from each other by cross-walls. (Life size: 3/4 inch)

116

Adult bumblebees are heavy-bodied and covered with hair. Here a bumblebee sips nectar from a flower. (Life size: 3/4 inch)

FAMILY BOMBIDAE—THE BUMBLEBEES

These large heavy-bodied bees are common almost everywhere. They are colonial in habits, their colonies consisting of a dozen or so workers and the queen. Their bodies are very hairy, and colored black and yellow. Only the mated queens survive the winter, hibernating in hollow trees or in the ground. They emerge in spring and seek old mouse nests or similar places. Each queen, having found a suitable place, gathers pollen and nectar and stores it in the nest. She then lays eggs in it. These soon hatch into white, legless larvae that feed upon the mixture of food. The queen continues to collect food and to lay more eggs. The adult bumblebees that soon mature are all workers and smaller than their mother. They set about enlarging the nest, gathering food, and other duties. In time, more workers are produced. Near summer's end, new queens and some drones are produced; all the rest eventually die. Only the mated queens survive the winter.

Below: Wax cells of a bumblebee nest. Two cells have been broken open to show pupal bees. (Life size: 3/4 inch) Right: Close-up of a bumblebee pupa in its cell. It is nearly ready to change into the adult stage. (Life size: 3/4 inch)

FAMILY APIDAE—THE HONEYBEES

These industrious insects have been under human domestication for thousands of years and nearly everyone is familiar with the delicious honey they produce. They also produce wax, used in a wide variety of products.

In many ways the lives of honeybees *(Apis mellifera)* are similar to those of bumblebees. However, their colonies are much larger, consisting of thousands of workers and one queen. The queen and workers (imperfect females) all result from fertilized eggs. Males or drones are present at certain times and these result from unfertilized eggs. The workers are actually undeveloped females and cannot mate. They may sometimes lay eggs but these eggs produce only drones.

Honeybee larvae are reared in wax comb containing numerous cells. They are white, legless, and are cared for and fed by young workers called "nurse bees." After serving for a certain period in this capacity, the nurse bees graduate to field work consisting of gathering pollen and nectar from flowers.

When the larvae are mature, their wax cells are capped and they change into pupae. In time, they change into adults and gnaw their way out of their cells. Their lives of toil then begin.

Adult honeybee worker collecting pollen from a passion flower. Note the filled pollen baskets on her hind legs. (Life size: 1/2 inch)

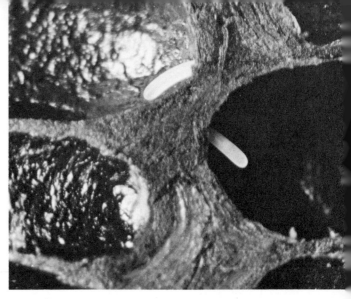

This view inside a honeybee hive shows a number of workers and a drone (center). The workers are feeding larval bees in their wax cells. (Life size, workers: 1/2 inch)

This is a cross-section through a honeybee wax comb showing newly laid eggs in the wax cells. (Life size, eggs: 1/16 inch)

The queen's only duty is that of egg-laying; she is cared for and fed by the workers.

Under certain conditions, usually when the hive becomes crowded, special cells are built in which the queen lays fertilized eggs that will develop into new queens. The first queen to emerge from her cell destroys all the other queens in their cells. Other special cells are also built, and in these the old queen lays eggs destined to develop into drones. Shortly, the young queen and drones fly out of the hive and mating occurs. The mated queen then returns to the hive. Within a short time the old queen leaves the hive, taking a "swarm" of workers with her. They will establish a new colony in a hollow tree or in some other suitable location. Thus does the chain of honeybee life continue.

Page numbers in **boldface** *are those on which illustrations appear*

125

THE AUTHOR-PHOTOGRAPHER

Entomologist Ross E. HUTCHINS is also an expert nature photographer, and this combination of interests has resulted in more than thirty years of studying, photographing and writing about insects, plants, animals and birds. Born in Montana, he grew up on a cattle ranch near Yellowstone Park. At Montana State College he majored in biological sciences and later he received his Ph.D. in zoology and entomology from Iowa State College.

Dr. Hutchins' articles and pictures of natural history subjects have appeared in encyclopedias, books, and magazines, including European publications. His most recent adult book was *Hidden Valley of the Smokies*, a naturalist's adventure in the Great Smoky Mountains. His many juvenile titles include *The Bug Clan, Grasshoppers and Their Kin, The World of Dragonflies and Damselflies, The Ant Realm, Galls and Gall Insects, Plants Without Leaves, Caddis Insects,* and *This Is a Tree.* All are noted for their remarkable close-up photographs by the author.

Ross Hutchins, for many years Director of the State Plant Board of Mississippi and Professor Emeritus of Entomology at Mississippi State University, lives in Mississippi, devoting his time to travel, writing, and photographing plant and animal life. He is listed in *Who's Who* and *American Men of Science.*